History's Greatest Unsolved Mysteries

Exploring The World's Most Intriguing Secrets For Young Readers

Lane Park

Contents

Introduction   v

1. The Lost City of Atlantis   1
2. The Pyramids of Egypt   8
3. The Bermuda Triangle   16
4. Stonehenge   23
5. The Nazca Lines   31
6. The Mystery of Roanoke Colony   39
7. The Shroud of Turin   45
8. The Voynich Manuscript   52
9. The Amber Room   59
10. Jack the Ripper   65
11. The Loch Ness Monster   73

Conclusion   79
References   83

Introduction

Ever sat in a room, the weight of a story from the past heavy in the air, and felt that itch? That deep-rooted curiosity to dig deeper, to find answers that seem just out of reach? History, with its vast landscapes of tales and epochs, has always beckoned the curious, challenging us with puzzles that refuse to be neatly wrapped up.

Think of the Egyptian pyramids standing tall against the sands of time or the enigmatic smile of Mona Lisa, holding secrets perhaps only she knows. These aren't just tales; they're puzzles, challenges, a silent dare to all those who chance upon them. They remind us that history isn't just about dates and events—it's alive with mysteries waiting for someone brave enough to solve them.

Why do these mysteries matter? Because they remind us that every era, every civilization, has its enigmas. These unsolved tales are the knots in the fabric of history, urging us to pull and unravel, to understand the bigger picture. They're not just stories; they're gateways into understanding human nature, the intricate dance of fate and chance, and the universal quest for meaning.

Picture yourself as a detective amid the enormous halls of time, rather than the busy streets of a modern metropolis. That's what this adventure provides. It is about providing you with the skills and state of mind to walk in the footsteps of history's sleuths. You'll travel across time, decipher ancient inscriptions, and interact with tales that have left even the most knowledgeable researchers perplexed.

You will not simply read these pages; you will research. Each mystery will push you, tickle your mind, and entice you to go deeper. It is not about knowing all of the answers, but about enjoying the excitement of the quest, the thrill of discovery, and the awe of the unknown.

Introduction

So, with intrigue as your guide and history as your playing field, let us go on this exciting adventure. The world's fascinating mysteries are waiting to be revealed.

Chapter 1
The Lost City of Atlantis

Imagine an ancient era when legends of a mystical island named Atlantis thrived. This island, according to tales, was beyond magnificent. It was a city of elegant buildings, huge palaces, and lively streets. But Atlantis was no ordinary island; it was enormous, spanning lands and seas and ringed by the powerful Atlantic Ocean.

The legend claims that Atlantis received its name from Atlas, a great god. His father, Poseidon, the lord of the waters, appointed him king of this magnificent realm. Atlantis was like a paradise, with its gold and silver treasures and unusual animals. The primary city in the center of Atlantis was supposed to be the most beautiful, with sky-high architecture.

But not everything was flawless. The people of Atlantis grew proud and greedy. They started to believe they were above everyone else. This enraged the gods, particularly Zeus, the most powerful of them all. The gods chose to punish Atlantis for its arrogant behavior and the battles it caused.

One fateful day, the ground trembled and the seas exploded. Atlantis started to sink. Wave after wave broke across its beaches, and the entire island vanished beneath the water. The once-great city of Atlantis vanished forever.

When Did We First Hear About Atlantis?

Around 360 B.C., an intelligent Greek philosopher by the name of Plato became the first person to share this tale. He discussed Atlantis in his works of literature, *Timaeus* and *Critias*. Plato characterized Atlantis as an island of beauty and wonder but warned against the perils of greed and arrogance.

Many people now doubt if Atlantis truly existed or if it was just a tale. However, one thing is certain: the mythology of Atlantis continues to captivate our imaginations, reminding us of the strength of nature and the costs of our decisions.

Historical Accounts and Theories

Plato, the ancient Greek thinker, painted a vivid picture of Atlantis. He described it as a landmass bigger than modern-day northern Africa and a big chunk of Turkey combined! If Atlantis truly existed and was submerged underwater in the Atlantic, we'd surely see it on our modern-day underwater maps.

But why do so many people believe in this lost city? A big reason is Ignatius Donnelly. In the 1880s, he wrote a ground-breaking book suggesting that Atlantis was real and was a peaceful haven for early humans. He believed that Atlantis inspired many of the great ancient civilizations (Giller, 2022).

Interestingly, Donnelly's ideas were influenced by a discovery in the 1870s. An enthusiast used ancient texts to locate the city of Troy, a place once thought to be purely legendary. Donnelly's ideas sparked a wave of interest, making people wonder: if there was a real Troy, as some believed, why couldn't Atlantis be real too?

James Romm, a classics professor, says the tale of Atlantis is simply captivating. It's packed with elements that stir our imagination and make us dream. Plato's Atlantis was no ordinary city. It was founded by beings who were half god and half human. They built a splendid civilization, surrounded by rings of land and water, with a grand city at its heart. Imagine streets lined with gold and silver, and a landscape teeming with rare wildlife!

Now, where could this magnificent city have been? The theories are endless! Some say it was in the Mediterranean, others near Spain, or even as far as Antarctica. Charles Orser, a history curator, notes that almost every imaginable spot on the map has been suggested as Atlantis's location (Drye, 2017).

While many legends and stories mention Atlantis, Plato's writings remain the primary source. He spoke of Atlantis as if it existed 9,000 years before his time. But here's the thing: Most scientists doubt its existence. Even Robert Ballard, the explorer who found the Titanic, says there's no hard evidence for Atlantis.

However, Ballard adds a twist. He believes that, while Atlantis might be a myth, it could've been inspired by real events. About 3,600 years ago, a massive volcano blew up on the island of Santorini, near Greece (Mambra, 2023). This event wiped out the advanced Minoan civilization. The timing doesn't match Plato's tale, but it's intriguing.

Romm thinks Plato crafted the Atlantis story to explore deep philosophical ideas. For him, Atlantis was a symbol of a society that lost its way, consumed by greed and moral decay. The gods, angered by this, supposedly punished Atlantis with catastrophic destruction.

In later centuries, especially after Columbus discovered America, many thought the New World might be Atlantis. The 20th and 21st centuries saw even more theories. One particularly buzzworthy claim in 2018 suggested that Atlantis was found! But it turned out to be a misunderstanding about some modern experimental ponds in Spain.

So, the mystery continues. Was Atlantis just a tale, or did it once stand tall, only to be swallowed by the sea? The quest for answers keeps historians, scientists, and dreamers intrigued, searching for clues to one of history's greatest enigmas.

Possible Locations and Why It Fascinates Us

The allure of Atlantis is so strong that, despite being largely considered a myth, it has captured imaginations for centuries. The quest to locate this legendary city has led to theories that span continents and oceans. From the chilly waters of Antarctica to the sunny coasts of the Caribbean, Atlantis has been "found" in numerous places. Yet Plato's ancient writings offer some clues.

Plato described Atlantis as lying beyond the Pillars of Hercules, which are believed to be the Strait of Gibraltar. This places the lost city somewhere in the vast expanse of the Atlantic Ocean. But with advancements in technology and research, several spots have been proposed:

- **Spain:** Near Cadiz, explorers using satellite images believe they've located Atlantis, with nearby cities possibly built by its survivors.
- **Off Africa:** A city-like shape spotted online led to Atlantis speculations, but experts later dismissed it as a sea pattern.
- **Greece:** The ancient volcanic eruption on Santorini has some believing it inspired Plato's tales of Atlantis.
- **Cyprus:** In 2004, underwater structures resembling Plato's descriptions were found near Cyprus, reigniting interest.

The fascination with Atlantis isn't just about locating a lost city. It's a quest to understand our past, explore ancient civilizations, and perhaps uncover truths hidden beneath layers of myth and legend. Until concrete evidence emerges, Atlantis will remain one of history's most captivating enigmas, drawing adventurers, researchers, and dreamers into its watery depths.

Modern Interpretations and Explorations

Even though there's no real proof that Atlantis existed, many are still seeking to find it, sometimes assuming that archeologists are hiding evidence. But these ideas have been mostly dismissed as untrue.

Modern explorers, armed with fancy technology, have dived deep into the ocean to find Atlantis. While they've discovered some interesting stuff, they haven't found anything to point toward the lost city, leaving Atlantis still a big mystery.

But Atlantis isn't just a puzzle for scientists. People have been inspired by Atlantis in lots of ways. From books to paintings to songs, it's a symbol of a lost, amazingly advanced city. It's everywhere in stories, movies, and games. Famous authors like Jules Verne and H.G. Wells wrote about it. And if you've seen Disney's *Atlantis: The Lost Empire* or *Aquaman* from 2018, you've encountered Atlantis in movies! Even if it might not be real, it sparks our imagination.

Beyond the fun stuff, the experts—like archaeologists and historians—are still debating if Atlantis was a thing. Some say it's a mix of myths, old-timey misunderstandings, and big ideas from the past.

As time has passed, we have seen Atlantis in different ways. Some see it as a warning about being too powerful and ambitious. Others dream of Atlantis as a perfect place, full of knowledge and peace. But mostly, Atlantis teaches us about our fascination with things we don't know. It's like a big question mark in history. And even with limited proof, we love to explore and guess about it.

So, the mystery of Atlantis lives on, making us wonder about the past, stories, and our own dreams. Whether it was all made up by Plato, a lesson about being too proud, or a lost city we just can't find, Atlantis keeps our curiosity alive, just like its legend that ripples through our thoughts and fascinations.

Chapter 2
The Pyramids of Egypt

A long, long time ago, in the marvelous territory of Egypt, a series of truly remarkable structures were built: the Pyramids of Egypt! Picture large, soaring buildings made out of enormous blocks that have held firm for almost 4,000 years. These magnificent masterpieces were constructed at a time when Egypt was regarded as civilization's star, and those who lived there built them to display their might and fortune.

Now, why did they make these giant wonders? Well, they weren't just big piles of rocks—they were actually gigantic tombs for special people called pharaohs. Pharaohs were like the kings of ancient Egypt, and they believed that after they left this world, they would turn into powerful gods in another realm. So, they wanted to make sure they had these incredibly elegant tombs filled with all the precious things they might need in the afterlife.

The first pyramid was started by Pharaoh Khufu around 2550 B.C.—that's a really, really long time ago! His son, Pharaoh Khafre, figured he'd like one for himself and built the second pyramid around 2520 B.C. And though this one was a little smaller, it was made unique by a mysterious statue that was built to guard his tomb. This statue, called the Sphinx, was like having a magical guardian for your treasure!

Then Pharaoh Menkaure decided to join the trend and built the third one in 2490 B.C. It was smaller than the first two, but it had a luxurious interior. These pyramids, especially the famous ones in Giza, have been like gigantic time-travel machines, letting us peek into Egypt's fascinating past.

Now, here's the exciting part: More than 100 pyramids have been discovered in Egypt! They come in all shapes and sizes, like the early stepped pyramid of Djoser and the uniquely shaped Bent Pyramid. But the three Pyramids of Giza are like the rock stars of the pyramid world, standing tall and proud on the west bank of the Nile River.

People have been fascinated by these incredible structures for centuries. There have been brave explorers clearing sand and exploring secret chambers inside the pyramids. Some even used dynamite, which creates explosions, to uncover their secrets! Luckily, clever archaeologists came along later, scanning and restoring these ancient wonders.

But here's the mystery: Even with all this exploring and studying, many secrets of the pyramids remain unsolved. It's a puzzle waiting for curious minds to unravel it.

How Were They Built? Theories and Evidence

In ancient Egypt, the builders of the pyramids were like superheroes—skilled workers living in a temporary city near the construction site, covering a whopping 17 acres. Archaeological findings, including bakeries and animal bones, reveal they were well-fed, creating a super-organized community backed by a strong central authority.

The mystery deepens as scientists and engineers today puzzle over how the ancient Egyptians achieved this monumental task, especially with the Great Pyramid's 2.3 million blocks of limestone and granite, each weighing at least two tons. One theory proposes sleds and wet sand as tools for moving massive stones, with a physicist discovering that wet sand reduces friction, making it easier to slide heavy objects.

But how were these blocks lifted for the pyramid's construction? A steep quarry ramp suggests stones were pulled up slopes, potentially using exterior ramps spiraling like a mountain road. The intrigue heightens with the use of sleds, wooden rollers, or posts for turning blocks into rollable shapes, like barrels of wizard's brew.

Recent findings add another layer to the mystery, suggesting the ancient Egyptians used a Nile River branch to transport massive stones. Researchers tested fossilized soil samples, uncovering evidence of the Khufu Branch, an ancient waterway that aided in stone transportation. This revelation, inspired by an ancient papyrus found in the Red Sea, acts like a secret scroll guiding researchers to the hidden river route.

The pyramid construction wasn't just about stacking blocks; it was a grand national project involving communities across Egypt. Even today, scientists and engineers act as detectives, debating and searching for the pyramid's construction secrets. Future technology might unveil hidden chambers and blueprints, completing the final chapter of this captivating ancient Egyptian tale (Shuttleworth, 2023).

Secrets of the Pharaohs and Their Tombs

These structures, beyond being grand pyramids, serve as enchanted books recounting the tales of ancient Egyptian kings. Like time-traveling detectives, scientists have unveiled hidden rooms and chambers within, with recent revelations in the Great Pyramid of Giza introducing secret passageways and a mysterious void, deepening the enigma.

Journey back to the third and fourth dynasties of the Old Kingdom, an era when Egypt radiated with prosperity. The kings, perceived as real-life fantastical beings between humans and gods, were chosen by mighty deities as earthly representatives. Posthumously, these kings embarked on a cosmic journey, transforming into Osiris, the god of the dead, while the new pharaoh assumed the role of Horus, the falcon god, protecting Ra, the sun god.

Imagine the pyramids as magical staircases for the king's soul to ascend to heaven. The angled sides symbolized the sun's rays, guiding the king to join the gods, especially Ra. The ancient Egyptians believed the king's spirit, called "ka," lingered with his body after death. To care for this spirit, the king's mummified body, along with gold vessels, food, furniture, and offerings, was buried.

Here's the twist in the tale: the pyramids weren't merely fancy resting places but the heart of a cult honoring the deceased king, designed to endure for his family, officials, and priests interred nearby.

The secrets of the tombs don't conclude there. Enter the Curse of the Pharaohs, a magical deterrent for tomb disturbers. Legends spun tales of curses befalling violators with terrible tragedies and misfortunes.

Archaeologists and treasure hunters faced these mythical curses, with stories circulating about misfortunes for those daring to open ancient tombs. However, it's crucial to note: These stories lean toward myths rather than proven facts. No scientific evidence supports the existence of these curses.

Despite the lack of proof, these myths endure through centuries, captivating minds and adding an air of mystery to ancient Egyptian tombs. They also play a crucial role in protecting these historical sites from looting, ensuring the treasures within continue to whisper enchanting tales of the past.

Discoveries That Still Surprise Us

The pyramids stand like ancient guardians, their mysteries revealing themselves slowly to those who seek their secrets. Scholars, over time, have unveiled surprising facts about ancient Egypt through these timeless structures, blending technical prowess with mythology and superstition. These pyramids, indestructible pieces of architecture, continue to hold untold stories, proving that there's always more to discover beneath their majestic surface.

- **Celestial alignment:** Imagine the stars guiding the construction of the pyramids! In the year 2000, a brilliant British Egyptologist named Kate Spence discovered that the Big Dipper and Little Dipper were like cosmic compasses, guiding the pyramids to align in a perfect north-south direction. It's like connecting the dots in the night sky to create these colossal wonders. Imagine ancient builders gazing at the dotted sky, connecting their earthly wonders to the stars above!

- **The truth of the builders:** Many had drawn the conclusion that the pyramids were built by slaves. Thanks to the Greek historian Herodotus, this notion spread like wildfire and was depicted in Hollywood movies too. But this might not be true at all. In the 1990s, the tombs of pyramid builders were uncovered. These tombs revealed that the builders were not slaves but skilled individuals from lower-income families. Their tomb burials show that their pyramid-building role was an honor, not a form of punishment. These builders were gifted architects, measuring with such precision that their margin of error was only up to 0.05 degrees. Imagine being so perfect in your work that you could date the pyramids using astronomical records. It's like ancient Egyptian builders had a secret language with the stars!

- **It tells time:** The Great Pyramid isn't just a colossal structure; it's a time-telling masterpiece. Picture a giant sundial casting shadows on carefully marked stones, telling time, signaling solstices, and even helping the Egyptians define the solar year. It's like a colossal clock that not only tells the hour but also dances with the rhythms of the sun.

- **An endless field of secrets:** Egyptology, the study of all things ancient Egypt, is an ongoing adventure. Forget just reading inscriptions; researchers are using technology to excavate and solve the remaining mysteries. Picture stumbling upon a 4,500-year-old ramp near Luxor, giving clues about how the ancient Egyptians moved massive stones. And close to the

Saqqara burial site, a tomb revealed cat mummies
and wooden cat statues, adding to the treasure trove
of ancient wonders waiting to be explored.

The allure of ancient Egyptian tombs and their secrets has
enchanted generations. Despite the efforts of archaeologists
and historians, there's still much we don't know about the
ancient Egyptians and their beliefs. Many tombs remain
undiscovered, promising hidden secrets and treasures. Even
the ones we've found hold mysteries waiting to be unraveled.

Myths and legends, like the curse of the pharaohs, continue to
weave an air of mystery around these tombs, fueling our
fascination with ancient Egypt. The tombs are more than
stone structures; they are living testaments to the complexity
and sophistication of the ancient Egyptian civilization. The
secrets they contain, shrouded in magic and wonder, continue
to captivate and intrigue people around the world. The adventure into ancient Egypt's rich history is boundless and ever
evolving, leaving us eager for the next chapter of discovery.

Chapter 3
The Bermuda Triangle

For many years, sailors, explorers, and adventure seekers have been fascinated by a region in the vast and wonderful Atlantic Ocean. It's known as the Bermuda Triangle, a mysterious area off the southeastern coast of Florida that is about the size of 500,000 soccer fields.

Imagine sailing through this magical triangle. Some people have said that strange things happen here—like ships vanishing without a trace or planes disappearing into thin air! Can you believe that? It's like a mystery novel, but in the real world!

People have come up with all sorts of wild ideas to explain these mysterious happenings. Some think aliens are swooping down and taking things away for their own curious studies. Others believe the lost city of Atlantis (ring a bell?)—the mythical place—might be playing tricks on us from the deep sea. Some say there are secret whirlpools sucking ships and planes into different dimensions! It sounds like something out of a cool science fiction story, right?

Here's another mysterious detail about the Bermuda Triangle: It involves compasses. You know those magical tools that point north? Well, sometimes in the Bermuda Triangle, they get a bit confused. Instead of pointing to true north, they might point to magnetic north. What's the difference? Let me break it down for you. Normally, a compass would point to the North Pole, which is "true north." But in the Bermuda Triangle, it might get sneaky and point to a wandering spot called "magnetic north," where the Earth's magnetic field dives down like a secret tunnel into the planet! It's like the compass is playing its own little game of hide-and-seek!

But here's the deal: While the Bermuda Triangle sounds really mysterious, there is no official map that says, "You're inside the Bermuda Triangle!" The professional people who create official maps don't even call it the Bermuda Triangle; instead, they view it as part of the gigantic ocean.

The Bermuda Triangle may not even be a mystical passageway or a secret alien base. It may just be a section of water where nature throws curveballs, and sailors must be cautious. Remember that the ocean is a magnificent but often tricky place, whether you're sailing across the Bermuda Triangle or discovering other regions of the vast blue sea!

Famous Disappearances: Stories and Theories

Strange incidents and mysterious disappearances in this curious area off the southeastern edge of Florida have puzzled the world. These legends revolve around ghost ships and missing crews, all set against the waters of the rumored Bermuda Triangle. Are they just oceanic myths, or is there anything actually spooky going on?

1. *Ellen Austin* **and the Ghost Ship:** Back in 1881, a brave ship named *Ellen Austin* sailed through the stormy waters of the Bermuda Triangle. The captain, Griffin, spotted a mysterious ship sailing strangely in the distance. Thinking it might be a trap, Griffin kept a safe distance for two days. When his crew finally investigated, they found the other ship abandoned, with cargo untouched. Griffin decided to sail both ships to New York, but a storm separated them. When the storm cleared, the mysterious ship was once again lost, never to be seen again.

2. *Mary Celeste* **and the Vanishing Crew:** In 1872, the *Mary Celeste* was found adrift in the Atlantic, far from its intended route. Everything seemed normal, except the crew was missing. No trace of the captain, his family, or the crew was ever found. Theories ranged from criminal conspiracies to alien abductions and giant squids. Some even suggested the Bermuda Triangle played a part, but the mystery

remains unsolved. Why would a skilled crew abandon their ship on a clear day without a single clue?

3. **USS *Cyclops* and the Naval Enigma:** In 1918, the USS *Cyclops*, a mighty ship, vanished on its way to Baltimore. With no distress signals and fair weather reported, the ship and its 305 crew members disappeared without a trace. No wreckage, no SOS messages—just an eerie silence. To this day, it remains the largest loss of life in U.S. naval history, leaving everyone wondering what mysterious force could make a ship disappear.

4. *Witchcraft*, **the Unsinkable Cruiser:** A luxurious cruiser named *Witchcraft* left Miami in 1967 for a Christmas lights tour. Just a mile offshore, the captain called the Coast Guard, claiming a minor collision. But when help arrived in less than 20 minutes, *Witchcraft* was nowhere to be found. This unsinkable ship, equipped with life-saving gear, vanished without a trace. No signs of damage, no crew, just an empty sea. What could make a ship disappear so quickly and completely?

5. **The Aerial Mystery of Flight 19/PBM Mariner:** In 1945, Flight 19, a group of bomber planes, vanished over the Bermuda Triangle. Confused by compass malfunctions, they faced trouble in the stormy skies. Their transmissions faded, and despite a rescue effort, no wreckage or crew were ever found. Adding to the mystery, a search plane, the PBM Mariner, also disappeared. The Bermuda Triangle seemed to swallow them whole, leaving everyone puzzled.

Theories: Unraveling the Mystery

Why do ships and planes vanish in the Bermuda Triangle? Some say supernatural forces, but science points to geophysical and environmental factors. Navigation errors near the agonic line, powerful rogue waves, and converging storms may be the culprits. The U.S. National Oceanic and Atmospheric Administration assures us that these mysterious disappearances aren't more frequent here than in any other part of the ocean (Luebering, 2024). The Bermuda Triangle's secrets continue to captivate, but science suggests it's just another part of the vast, mysterious sea.

Between Myth and Reality: Scientific Perspectives

While stories of vanishing ships and planes have added a sprinkle of mystery and fantasy to the tales, there's a whole world of science waiting to be discovered! Now, the first thing to know is that many believe the mysteries of the Bermuda Triangle are more like tricky puzzles than ghostly tales. You see, people love a good mystery, because sometimes the truth might not be as exciting as the stories we hear. But think about it; if science can make reality feel so mysterious, isn't that super cool? What a fascinating world we live in! How many secrets might be out there, waiting to be discovered?

So here's some real science that could be behind the mystery:

1. **Navigational Nudges:** The Bermuda Triangle is like a busy highway for ships and planes. With so much traffic, accidents are bound to happen. Hurricanes and unpredictable weather dance in this region,

making it a challenging place to sail or fly. Sometimes, when the sea gets rough, ships might meet a stormy end.

2. **Magnetic Magic:** Remember the compass trickery we mentioned? Well, there might actually be an explanation behind it! The Earth's magnetic north isn't exactly where the maps say it is. This difference can confuse sailors, especially near the agonic line, which is a hidden boundary in the Bermuda Triangle. This boundary is where magnetic north and the geographic North Pole line up perfectly, making compasses go, "Wait a minute, which way is true north?" So, when sailors sail near this agonic line, their compasses might start playing tricks on them. It's nature's little trick that can lead boats off course, especially in the shallow, island-filled Caribbean Sea.

3. **Bubble Trouble:** Now, here's a crazy fact: Massive bubbles from underwater gas could gobble up ships! Scary, I know! Some scientists think that methane bubbles might escape from the ocean floor, turning the water into a bubbly mess. But don't worry. There's no recent proof of this happening in the Bermuda Triangle, at least not since 15,000 years ago!

4. **Rogue Wave Riddles:** Picture gigantic waves that take everyone by surprise! Rogue waves can be like ocean monsters, rising way higher than their fellow waves. Some scientists say that if a ship gets caught between these waves, it might snap in half like a cracker (Scharping, 2024)! However, there's no concrete proof that rogue waves are behind the mysteries we've heard about.

And here's a piece of information you might find interesting: When we look at all the traffic passing through, the Bermuda Triangle doesn't have more accidents than any other busy part of the world. It's all like a puzzle with missing pieces, and science is helping us put it all together.

The Bermuda Triangle in Popular Culture

The Bermuda Triangle, a region associated with tales of vanished ships and planes, captured public imagination in the 1960s. The term gained popularity as magazines highlighted the unusual number of losses in the stretch between Bermuda, Miami, and Puerto Rico. The 1970s saw a surge of interest fueled by Charlie Berlitz's bestselling 1969 novel, *The Bermuda Triangle*. The book, featuring UFOs and the lost city of Atlantis, became a cultural sensation, selling 30 million copies and shaping popular perceptions of the mystery.

However, beneath the waves, the reality of the Atlantic Ocean differs. Busy waters are prone to accidents, especially with storms like cyclones and hurricanes. The enduring myth of the Bermuda Triangle is less about facts and more about the allure of the unexplained, the mysterious, and the fantastical.

In truth, the secret of the Bermuda Triangle may not lie in the waves but in our perception and recollection of the tales. Our minds, akin to adventurous storytellers, often prefer the extraordinary, creating a mysterious aura around this fascinating corner of the world. As we navigate the unknown, it's essential to seek truth, balance mystery with reality, and not get too lost in the allure of the unknown. Life itself is a beautiful blend of mystery, fantasy, and reality.

Chapter 4
Stonehenge

Once upon a time, in a land steeped in ancient wonders, there existed a captivating circle of stones known as Stonehenge. This extraordinary structure, nestled on England's Salisbury Plain in Wiltshire, serves as a mysterious portal to bygone times, unveiling the concealed tales of our ancestors from nearly 4,500 years ago.

Imagine a wide circle of gigantic stones, each one sturdily fashioned and defiantly standing the test of time. Stonehenge emerged around the same era as Egypt's Great Pyramid, marking an important period in British and European history characterized by amazing transformations. They're more than just rocks; they symbolize a time when humanity reshaped its connection with the land in ways that we can only imagine.

As you explore the site today, the giant stones still stand, arranged in a curious circular formation. But here's the thing: Stonehenge wasn't built in a day. No sir, it took many, many years and generations of ancient people to create this wonder.

Imagine 4,000 years ago, when Stonehenge had an outer circle of 30 standing stones called "sarsens." These encircled five gigantic stone arches in a horseshoe shape. Inside the outer circle and the horseshoe were two smaller circles made of "bluestones," and there were even four "station stones" hanging out just outside the central monument. The whole shebang was surrounded by a circular ditch and bank, and guess what? It's still there today!

Now, let's dive into the magical mystery: How on earth did they build Stonehenge? Well, my friend, that's a question that has puzzled people for centuries, and the answer is still as mysterious as ever. Legend has it that giants placed the stones on a mountain in Ireland, and a wizard named Merlin whisked them away to England. Too bad they didn't actually have a wizard back then—that would've made things way easier!

Here's the mind-boggling part: The bluestones, weighing as much as two cars each, traveled all the way from rock outcrops in Wales, about 225 kilometers away! How did they get there? Well, they might have been dragged on sledges to a waterway and floated on rafts to the building site. Talk about a stone's grand adventure!

Seriously, though, imagine lifting stones as heavy as four African elephants! That sounds crazy! Archaeologists believe the sarsen stones made a journey of 32 kilometers on big wooden sledges. But how did they stand those incredibly heavy boulders upright? It's like magic! But the truth of it might actually be even cooler than magic! Builders dug deep ditches, used ropes, strong wooden poles, and frames to actually lift the stones, and then filled the ditches with rocks and rubble to hold them steady. And voilà—Stonehenge was born! Incredible, right?

So, the next time you gaze upon the ancient wonder that is Stonehenge, remember the incredible journey these stones took and the magical mystery that surrounds them. It's like a real-life fairy tale written in rocks and standing tall for all of us to marvel at. The end—or is it just the beginning of Stonehenge's enchanting tale?

Who Built It and Why: Theories and Debates

The mystery of Stonehenge's builders has puzzled curious minds for ages. As the sun sets over Salisbury Plain, casting long shadows on the ancient stones, the tales of who erected this enigmatic monument weave through time like whispers in the wind.

Long before the bustling traffic on modern roads, Stonehenge stood witness to the footprints of early Mesolithic hunter-gatherers, who, it seems, were the first to modify the sacred site. These ancient wanderers left their mark, but the true architects of Stonehenge emerged later, during a time when powerful forces shaped the land.

In the pages of history, a 12th-century storyteller named Geoffrey of Monmouth spins a captivating yarn. According to him, Stonehenge's creation is entwined with the legendary wizard Merlin and the tragic tale of King Aureoles Ambrosias. In a bid to honor fallen nobles, a stone circle known as the Giants' Ring was sought from Ireland. Legends of magical African bluestones and Merlin's sorcery dance through this narrative, creating a tale that enchanted minds for centuries (Onion et al., 2010a).

However, as the sun rises on the truth, we discover that Stonehenge predates Merlin and the characters who inspired him by thousands of years. Early hypotheses tossed around names like Saxons, Danes, Romans, Greeks, or even Egyptians as the possible builders. The 17th-century archaeologist John Aubrey proposed the Druids, high priests of the Celts, as the masterminds behind Stonehenge. This theory gained traction, enduring for centuries and even influencing modern Druids, who gather at the site for solstices.

Yet, as science unfurls its findings, a more plausible theory emerges. Most scholars today agree that Stonehenge was a collaborative effort across three different tribes at distinct times. The saga begins around 3000 B.C. with the Windmill Hill people, Neolithic agrarians skilled in farming and imbued with a deep reverence for circles and symmetry. Their legacy is etched in the circular furrows of Windmill Hill and the large stone-encased tombs.

Enter the Beaker people, arriving around 2000 B.C. with their sophisticated ways. These sun worshipers, organized and warlike, aligned Stonehenge precisely with significant celestial events. Their arrival marked a shift toward metal implements and communal living, leaving traces of their culture in the burial mounds.

Finally, the Wessex Peoples, entering the scene around 1500 B.C. during the Bronze Age, brought advanced knowledge and precision. Masters of trade and calculation, they carved a bronze dagger on a sarsen stone, leaving their mark on Stonehenge's evolution into the marvel we see today (*Who Built Stonehenge?*, 2019).

As the sun continues its eternal dance over Stonehenge, the secrets of its builders remain woven into the very fabric of time, inviting us to explore the captivating chapters of our ancient past.

Astronomical Significance: Solstices and Alignments

In the magical world of Stonehenge, where the ancient stones stand as guardians of secrets, there lies a tale of astronomy and celestial wonder. Stonehenge isn't just a bunch of rocks; it's like an ancient observatory and a magical calculator rolled into one!

Long, long ago, when the 12th-century historian Geoffrey of Monmouth and the architect Inigo Jones were puzzling over Stonehenge, they had their own ideas. Some thought it was a

Roman ruin, others imagined the Druids as the master builders, and a few even believed it to be a wizard's creation.

But it was the 20th century that brought a new twist to the story. A wise solar physicist named Sir Joseph Norman Lockyer made accurate surveys and thought, "Hey, these builders must've known a thing or two about the stars!" This idea set the stage for the possibility that Stonehenge wasn't just a bunch of stones but a grand observatory (Chapman and Henbest, 2022).

As we venture into the mysteries of Stonehenge's purpose, we stumble upon the solstices—the times when the sun does its dance in the sky. Some folks thought Stonehenge was all about the summer solstice, but hold your horses; recent research suggests a twist!

You see, Stonehenge might not have been built for the bright days of summer but rather for the dark days of midwinter. As the sun played hide-and-seek in the winter sky, the ancient Britons might have celebrated the solstice when the days were at their darkest. It's like Stonehenge was a massive calendar, marking the changing seasons.

Now, if you stand right in the middle of Stonehenge and gaze toward the northeast, you'll catch a glimpse of the sun rising over the heel stone during midsummer. That's when the modern-day Druids gather to celebrate. But wait, Professor Clive Ruggles (1997) suggests a different twist—what if it's actually the midwinter sunset that was more important?

Imagine standing near the heel stone, looking back at Stonehenge. In the quiet hush of the winter solstice, you'd witness the sun setting behind the massive stone arches, creating a breathtaking view. It's like Stonehenge had a secret preference for the cozy darkness of winter nights.

The builders of Stonehenge, those wise folks from around 2500 B.C., might have had the midwinter solstice in mind when they arranged those giant stones. It's like they created a cosmic runway, guiding the sun's descent as the year turned. Archaeologists even found grooves in the Earth, remnants of an ancient natural runway that pointed toward the midwinter sunset.

And guess what? The nearby Neolithic settlement, Durrington Walls, spills its secrets too! Pigs' teeth tell tales of feasts around the midwinter solstice. So, perhaps Stonehenge wasn't just an ancient calculator; it was a festive hub where people gathered to feast and celebrate the magic of the changing seasons.

As the sun sets on Stonehenge, casting shadows that dance with ancient whispers, the true purpose of this mystical monument remains an ever-evolving tale, waiting to be discovered by those who dare to explore its celestial secrets.

Ongoing Mysteries and Discoveries

Stonehenge, a tale woven in ancient mysteries, continues to captivate with its enigmatic builders and the magical stones that stand tall. Imagine the Windmill Hill people crafting circles and tombs around 3000 B.C. Then came the Beaker people, sun worshippers from Europe around 2000 B.C., adding a celestial touch. The Wessex Peoples, in 1500 B.C., brought bronze daggers and precision to complete the masterpiece.

Now, the stones—the bluestones, mystical and weighing as much as two cars—can be traced back to Wales, 225 kilometers away. Dragged on sledges and floated on rafts, they embarked on an epic journey. The sarsen stones, as heavy as four African elephants, traveled 32 kilometers on wooden sledges. Picture the sweat and determination etched into every stone with hammers and chisels.

Yet mysteries persist. The purpose of Stonehenge, its celestial alignments, and the stories within the stones continue to captivate. As the sun sets, Stonehenge stands as a silent witness, inviting us to join the ongoing quest for understanding in this ancient tapestry of history.

Chapter 5
The Nazca Lines

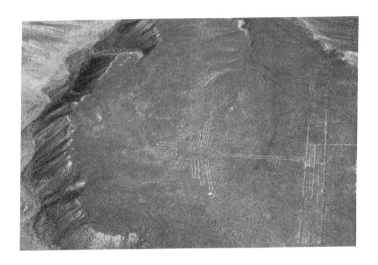

Viewed from above, the vast, dry plain of southern Peru, where rocks and sand reach as far as the eye can see, is given an amazing change. On a soaring aircraft, an endless array of tan and rust-red hues gives way to a canvas of white lines etched into the very center of the desert. These are the Nazca lines, an ancient mystery that has captivated curious minds for more than 80 years.

The scorched region, where rain is as rare as finding a needle in a haystack, comes to life with strange shapes. Geometric wonders become apparent, including trapezoids, rectangles, triangles, and swirls, to form a fascinating tapestry. And then, like characters in a cosmic storybook, the lines evolve into animals: a graceful hummingbird, a clever spider, and a mischievous monkey.

Welcome to the land of mystery, just a little over 200 miles southeast of Lima, near the modern town of Nazca. Over 800 straight lines, 300 geometric figures, and 70 animal and plant designs, known as biomorphs, grace this ancient canvas. The sheer scale is jaw-dropping, with some straight lines stretching up to 30 miles and biomorphs reaching lengths of 50 to 1,200 feet—taller than the Empire State Building!

Now, let's embark on a journey into the past. How did these lines come to be? What purpose did they serve? The answers remain elusive, wrapped in the enigmatic embrace of time. Imagine the scholars scratching their heads, wondering if ancient aliens had a hand in this celestial artwork. It's a cosmic puzzle that keeps historians and scientists on their toes.

As we explore this ancient playground, it's like flipping through the pages of a mystical encyclopedia. The Nazca people, who inhabited this region over a thousand years ago, left no written record of their intentions. Were the lines pathways for ceremonies or messages to the gods? Or perhaps a giant playground for the ancient Nazca children?

The mystery deepens as we gaze upon these colossal drawings. Were they navigational aids for the gods flying above or celestial maps guiding the Nazca people through the vast desert? The very desert that witnesses less rainfall in a year than your backyard garden in a week!

So, young explorer, as you dive into the pages of this ancient tale, let your imagination soar. The Nazca lines are not just etchings in the earth; they're whispers from the past, inviting you to unravel their secrets and become a time-traveling detective in the great desert mystery.

Deciphering the Lines: Possible Meanings

In the year 1926, a Peruvian archaeologist named Toribio Mejia Xesspe set out on a mission. His quest? To unlock the secrets hidden in this ancient desert of southern Peru. Imagine him, like an adventurous detective, carefully studying the mysterious patterns etched into the earth.

But here's the twist: These lines are sneaky. You can't spot them from down below; they're like earth's secret doodles meant for the eyes in the sky. It wasn't until the 1930s, when brave pilots soared above Peru in their flying machines, that the world discovered these colossal drawings. Imagine the excitement as the people gazed down from their planes, marveling at shapes that seemed to dance on the desert floor.

Our hero, American professor Paul Kosok, touched down at the foot of a Nazca line in 1941, just after the winter solstice when the sun dipped low. Immersed in his studies, he witnessed the sun setting, its golden rays perfectly aligning with the line, prompting Kosok to poeticize the vast desert canvas as "the largest astronomy book in the world" (Golomb, 2010). But the tale continues with Maria Reiche, the Lady of the Lines, who dedicated 40 years to unraveling

Nazca's mysteries. Armed with theories of cosmic calendars, she staunchly defended the geoglyphs, living near the desert as their guardian and fending off reckless visitors who could harm these ancient wonders.

So, what, really, was the purpose of these ancient drawings? Imagine the Nazca people thriving from A.D. 1 to 700, creating a gigantic chalkboard on the pampa. Lines crisscross, overlap, and connect together like an intricate design. Explorers believe that these lines, especially the straight ones and trapezoids, were not maps but pathways to rituals (Reinhard, 1986). Not just any rituals—rituals pleading with the gods for water and fertile crops.

The Nazca people, it seems, used the lines not as directions but as cosmic connections. The trapezoids, those wide open spaces, were like doorways for people to enter and exit. And what were these rituals about? Picture ancient ceremonies where the Nazca people, with a humble heart, sought to satisfy the gods and ask for the life-giving gift of water.

But wait, that's not all! Animal friends join the cosmic drawings. Spiders, believed to bring rain; hummingbirds, spreading fertility; and monkeys, symbols of water-rich lands in the Amazon. The Nazca lines, it appears, were a grand plea to the heavens for the essentials of life.

Remember that the Nazca lines are a puzzle waiting to be solved. With every passing day, new technology and discoveries add layers to our understanding. So, keep your eyes open, for the story of the Nazca lines is still unfolding, and you might just be the one to crack the cosmic code!

How Were They Made? Techniques and Tools

The ingenious minds behind the Nazca Lines were likely the Nazca culture, although the Chavin and Paracas cultures, predating the Nazca, might have lent their hands to some of these wonders. Picture a vast canvas in the desert plains of the Rio Grande de Nazca river basin—an archaeological playground spreading over 75,000 hectares, one of the driest spots on our Earthly map.

Imagine the desert floor covered in a blanket of iron oxide-coated pebbles, painting the landscape a deep rust color. The ancient artists, armed with creativity, crafted their designs by skillfully removing the top 12 to 15 inches of rock, exposing the lighter-colored sand beneath. It's like revealing a hidden treasure with each block removed. Starting with small-scale models, they carefully scaled up their creations, transforming the desert floor into an ancient art gallery filled with big wonders.

Here's the secret technique: Most geoglyphs were formed by delicately removing rocks only from the border of the figures, creating a sort of outline. Others, however, were shaped by removing rocks from the inside, giving life to intricate details within the grand designs.

Imagine a vast, timeless canvas exposed to the elements. Rain, wind, and erosion usually play mischief with our outdoor creations, but not here. In this amazing desert, where raindrops are rarer than a treasure chest, the geoglyphs have stood tall throughout the ages. It's like a cosmic pact, ensuring that these ancient wonders remain largely unscathed, waiting for curious minds like yours to unlock the secrets they hold.

The Lines Today - Preservation and Ongoing Mystery

Unlike some ancient treasures around the world, these massive drawings have been spared from unintentional harm due to their remote location. But don't be too easily convinced, because the geoglyphs aren't completely immune to the challenges of the modern world.

Over the years, the Nazca have lines faced unexpected challenges. In 2009, rare rain showers, an unusual occurrence in the desert, left their mark on the geoglyphs as heavy downpours from the Pan-American Highway showered sand and clay onto a hand-shaped geoglyph. Five years later, Greenpeace unintentionally became vandals during a media stunt near the hummingbird geoglyph, leaving footprints on the rocks while promoting renewable energy. In 2018, a mischievous commercial truck driver drove onto the Nazca lines, etching deep scars into the desert canvas. These incidents raised concerns, prompting calls for increased security and surveillance to protect these ancient wonders from modern intrusions.

Preservation aside, the mystery of the Nazca lines remains largely unsolved. The purpose of the lines is still a riddle, a puzzle waiting to be solved. Some think they're linked to the heavens, representing constellations in the night sky. Others suggest a connection to aliens, adding a touch of extraterrestrial intrigue. And then, there's the idea of pilgrimage, with people walking across the lines to reach sacred places like Cahuachi and its adobe pyramids. Water, vital for life but elusive in the desert, could also be a key player in the lines' story, perhaps playing a role in ancient water-based rituals.

Some out-of-the-box theories have also popped up, like the idea of the Nazca people using balloons to observe the lines from above, though there's no archaeological evidence for this airborne adventure. But how could they create these humongous drawings without actually being able to see them? To this day, we don't know for sure. Mind-twisting, I know! The truth is, many archaeologists and scientists have studied the lines, but some pieces of the puzzle are still missing. There are unanswered questions—what are the lines for, who built them, and when were they built?

Despite the mystery, here's what's amazing: Thanks to ancient cultures, we can still marvel at the Nazca lines today. It's not just a popular tour in the air; it's a window into the incredible works of cultures older than the Incas. The lines are a journey back in time, inviting us to learn about the history of humanity before the conquerors arrived. So, as you stand in awe of these ancient wonders, remember that the Nazca lines are not just drawings on the ground; they're whispers from the past, calling you to communicate with the ancient people of Nazca.

Chapter 6
The Mystery of Roanoke Colony

Once upon a time, in the year 1587, a brave group of English settlers embarked on a grand adventure to Roanoke Island, off the coast of what we now call North Carolina. Their mission? To establish the very first permanent English outpost in the New World. Exciting, right?

There were around 115 of these settlers, and they were all determined to start over somewhere new. They had given this a shot before, two years earlier, but it wasn't exactly successful. Determined, they returned for another chance at creating history.

This adventurous mission was led by the new colony's governor, John White. Just as things were making progress, they began to run out of resources. So White had to sail back to England to gather supplies. But, oh dear, right as he arrived in England, a big naval war broke out between England and Spain. The Queen needed every ship for the mighty Spanish Armada face-off.

Fast forward to August of 1590, when John White finally returned to Roanoke. Imagine his shock and puzzlement when he found no sign of the settlement or its people! Where had they all gone? His wife, daughter, baby granddaughter (Virginia Dare, known for being the first English child born in the Americas), and the other migrants appeared to have disappeared into thin air.

There were no traces of violence or hints as to what had taken place, except for one strange word carved into a wooden post: "Croatoan." John White thought, "Aha! They must have moved to Croatoan Island, just 50 miles away." It sounded like a good plan, right? A fair assumption, yes. But, alas, when they searched the island, there was no sign of the missing colonists.

And so the mystery of the Roanoke Colony was born. What happened to those settlers? Why did they vanish without a trace? For generations, historians and explorers have struggled to solve this puzzle. The historical tale of Roanoke feels like a real-life treasure hunt, with hints and turns that keep everyone seeking answers. Will this mystery ever be solved? Only time will tell.

The Mysterious Disappearance: Clues and Theories

As the centuries passed, the mystery of the Roanoke Colony continued to baffle everyone, and people came up with all sorts of theories about what happened to the missing settlers.

One theory proposes that the Roanoke colonists faced attacks, either from Native Americans or the Spanish, due to the war between England and Spain, with a Spanish settlement in nearby St. Augustine, Florida. Another theory suggests harsh conditions, like starvation or disease, led to their unfortunate demise. In a more optimistic assumption, some believe the colonists may have joined a friendly Native American group, intermarrying and blending cultures, while an adventurous theory suggests survivors tried to sail back to England but faced challenges on their journey.

To unlock the secrets of this ancient puzzle, scientists and archaeologists have been hard at work. Some say the key might lie in multiple lines of evidence, including genetics. For this purpose, scientists have been studying the DNA of Native Americans in the area, looking for any signs of inter-marriage with the lost colonists.

Perhaps after the collapse of the Roanoke colony, the survivors split into different groups. In struggling colonial times, competing divisions often emerged, with some joining Native American groups and others attempting to survive independently.

The mystery of the Roanoke Colony continues to unfold, with each discovery bringing us closer to understanding the fate of those brave settlers. The adventure to solve this ancient puzzle marches on, fueled by the curiosity of historians, scientists, and young minds alike. What do you think might have happened to the Roanoke colonists? The answers may be hidden in the pages of history, waiting to be uncovered by the next generation of explorers and investigators.

Modern Theories and Archaeological Findings

In the 1930s and 1940s, someone found mysterious stones that claimed to spill the beans about the Roanoke colony's disappearance. These stones said Eleanor Dare, a colonist, wrote them and spilled the tea on what happened. But here's the twist—most experts think they're fake, like a tricky puzzle.

One stone, found in 1937 by a guy named Louis Hammond, talked about sad stuff, like Eleanor's family dying and problems with Native Americans. It hinted at a secret mass grave. But, surprise! It turned out that the other stones were fake, made by a crafty person named Bill Eberhardt.

People still wonder if the first stone is real due to its unique appearance. It's like a mystery inside a mystery. The Roanoke story keeps making people curious, leading to weird stories and tricks like these stones.

In 2012, researchers found a cool clue hidden in an old map in London. John White, who knew about Roanoke, had secretly drawn two forts, one where the colonists planned to move. The First Colony Foundation's team, like real-life detectives, checked a place in North Carolina near a Native American village in 2015. They found bits of European stuff, suggesting maybe Roanoke folks lived there.

In 2019, they looked at another place, finding more old pieces. These bits tell a story about people living there for a long time, maybe Roanoke friends. The missing English pipes, usually everywhere, make it even more interesting. The Roanoke mystery is like a never-ending adventure, with each discovery making it even more puzzling and exciting!

Historical Significance and Continued Fascination

For centuries, historians have been like detectives, trying to figure out what happened to the Roanoke colonists. Some thought they might have been quickly killed, while others believed they survived for twenty years, living among Native American groups like the Chowanocs and Weapemeocs, or maybe even the Chesapeakes. Jamestown settlers heard rumors about this, and during a big war, a guy named William Strachey said the chief of the Powhatan might have ordered them killed because he was worried they could team up with new settlers and cause trouble. Captain John Smith looked for them but never found any trace.

The Roanoke story has become a big legend in American history, like a really famous and mysterious tale. People often talk about the English discovering, being in charge, and then suddenly disappearing. John White's granddaughter, Virginia Dare, the first English baby born in North America, became a symbol of sorts, reminding us that Virginia's history starts earlier than Jamestown, down to the south. But there's something important to remember —the legend often forgets about the Native Americans of Ossomocumuck. Without them, the Roanoke colonists might not have survived. And while we talk a lot about the missing white colonists, it's also important to know that the Native Americans of the Ossomocumuck mostly disappeared too, facing changes brought by English and American cultures.

Chapter 7
The Shroud of Turin

Long ago, in the magical city of Turin, Italy, there was a mysterious cloth called the Shroud of Turin. This ancient piece of fabric, about 14 feet long and three feet wide, held a story that fascinated people worldwide.

The Shroud wasn't just any cloth—it carried the image of a man who had been crucified. Legend said it was the very cloth that was wrapped around Jesus Christ. Imagine a piece of fabric that touched the body of the man known for miracles and teachings. It was like a magical window, showing us a glimpse of Jesus' final moments.

So many questions surrounded the Shroud. How did this image appear? Was it made by a clever artist, or did it truly capture a moment in history? Could it be the face of Jesus imprinted on the fabric that once covered him?

Scientists dove into the mystery, spending countless hours studying and researching. Despite all their efforts, the Shroud remained a puzzle, keeping its secrets hidden. Woven from linen thread made from the flax plant's stems, the Shroud held echoes of a distant time. The threads were even finer than a human hair, adding to the magic of this ancient relic.

When the Shroud made rare appearances, millions gathered to see the images of the crucified man. It was like looking through a window into a time that shaped the beliefs of many.

And thus, the Shroud of Turin remained a captivating mystery, its secrets locked away by the fabric of time. The questions continued, and the quest to discover the truth went on, creating a story that traveled through centuries and captured the imagination of both young and old.

A Matter of Faith and Science: Analysis and Debates

As we dive into the fascinating world of the Shroud of Turin, we find ourselves in a place where science and faith come together. This old piece of cloth, with its mysterious double image of a man, acts like a bridge connecting the scientific world and the world of faith.

Looking at it from a scientific point of view, the Shroud is like a puzzle wrapped in linen. The double image, showing both the front and back of a man, has puzzled scientists for a long time. Even with all our fancy technology and studies, the Shroud remains a unique mystery. The bloodstains, wounds, water marks, and other mysterious signs challenge what we know about science. It's like a secret message written in fabric, just waiting to be figured out.

But for many people, especially in the Catholic Church, the Shroud is more than just an old piece of cloth. It's a special relic believed to have the imprint of Jesus Christ. They think the Shroud wrapped around Jesus, showing the marks from when he was crucified and even hints of when he came back to life. It's like a powerful connection to the heart of their Christian faith.

The Catholic Church, while understanding how important the Shroud is, doesn't officially say it's for sure Jesus' relic. They keep a balanced view, saying that whether it's real or not, the Shroud can inspire people on their spiritual journey.

Throughout history, many popes have talked about the Shroud with respect, seeing it as something that inspires rather than focusing on if it's real or not. Today, Pope Francis, the leader of the Catholic Church, continues this tradition. In 2013, he called the Shroud an "icon of a man scourged and crucified," saying it helps people think about the hard times Jesus went through. The Church sees the Shroud as a way for people to have their own special connection with the divine.

For those who believe, the Shroud isn't just an old thing; it's a way to feel close to their faith. It tells a story of sacrifice, redemption, and coming back to life. But for those who question and study, it's a big mystery—something that challenges us to think, explore, and maybe change how we understand history and the divine. The Shroud of Turin, mixing science and faith, remains a really interesting puzzle that goes beyond what we know in both worlds.

Historical Journey of the Shroud - From Past to Present

Let's travel back to ancient Edessa in the 2nd century, where an extraordinary cloth, once known as the Image of Edessa or the Mandylion (meaning "small cloth" or "towel" in Byzantine Greek), captured hearts. Many now believe this to be the same cloth that had the image of Christ, sparking speculation about the Mandylion's link to the Shroud of Turin, though we're still searching for solid proof.

Fast forward to 525 AD, when the Mandylion appeared from Edessa's walls after a flood. Its image was believed to have not been created by human hands and closely resembled the Shroud of Turin. In 944 AD, the Mandylion found a new home in Constantinople, proudly displayed in the Pharos Chapel. However, during the Fourth Crusade in 1204, chaos struck Constantinople, and the Shroud vanished, leaving a mystery that lasted for centuries.

The Shroud resurfaced in 1353, carried by French knight Geoffroi de Charny, marking the beginning of its documented existence. The years from 1204 to 1353 remain a puzzling gap, causing arguments among historians. In 1532, the Shroud survived a flaming challenge at Chambéry, France, with burn and water damage marks, proving its durability.

By 1578, the Shroud found a new home in Turin under Duke Emanuele Filiberto of Savoy. It became a revered relic, displayed on special occasions, and in 1694, it settled in the Chapel of the Holy Shroud in Turin Cathedral, captivating the world. In 1931, photographer Giuseppe Enri captured the Shroud's image, reigniting debates. The detailed imprint of a seemingly crucified man left everyone in awe.

The Shroud's journey weaves a tale of history, faith, and mystery, each stage adding to its rich tapestry. Unraveling its past, the Shroud of Turin remains a curious relic, standing the test of time and sparking curiosity in historians, theologians, and scientists alike.

Unanswered Questions and Ongoing Research

As we dig deeper into the story of the Shroud of Turin, we find ourselves standing at the crossroads of belief and skepticism, surrounded by unanswered questions that echo through the corridors of time.

Back in the 1980s, a special way of dating old things called radiocarbon dating hinted that the Shroud might be from medieval times, which surprised everyone. But wait, there's more to the story! Some people said the piece used for dating might be from a fix-up done later, not from the whole cloth. This mystery made the Shroud even more interesting. Another mystery is how the picture on the Shroud got there—was it a miracle or did an artist from a long time ago make it? People think it's tricky because the picture looks 3D and very detailed, which might have been too hard for someone from back then to do. Scientific tests, like looking at pollen and studying the fabric, give us some clues, but there's still more to figure out. The pollen found on the Shroud, traced to the Middle East, gives geographical evidence that makes it even more connected to the Bible stories.

Yet the most significant questions persist: Is the Shroud the authentic burial cloth of Jesus Christ, and could the images have been encoded onto the cloth by a burst of radiation emitted from his dead body? These questions, if answered as "yes," could have a huge impact on humanity, which means we should probably conduct the best scientific research possible.

The Shroud's uniqueness lies in its alleged imprint of a dead human body. In the realm of science, such an occurrence challenges our current understanding of physics, leaving us with an unexplored territory of possibilities.

In the end, the Shroud of Turin stands as a curious mystery, a tangible link to the divine for believers, and a captivating arti-fact for skeptics and scientists. It's not just a relic; it's a narrative that intertwines faith and science. Whether it's a masterpiece of medieval artistry or a sacred artifact, the Shroud invites us to journey beyond the limits of our beliefs and knowledge, acknowledging that some mysteries may forever elude our grasp.

Chapter 8
The Voynich Manuscript

Imagine stumbling upon a mysterious book filled with drawings of alien plants, naked women, strange objects, and zodiac symbols, all written in a language or code that no one can figure out. That's the Voynich Manuscript, and it's been puzzling people since 1912!

Let's go back to the 15th century, a time when knights and dragons roamed the lands. The Voynich Manuscript, named after a cool guy named Wilfrid M. Voynich, who found it, is like a time-traveling puzzle waiting to be solved. Imagine it as a magical diary with pages full of weird drawings in vibrant colors like green, brown, yellow, blue, and red.

Now, the drawings in this manuscript fall into six categories. First up, we have botanicals—113 plants that no one can identify. Next, there are drawings of the stars and planets, with symbols like fish, a bull, and even an archer. The third section is a bit odd—drawings of tiny, naked ladies doing mysterious things with tubes and capsules. Strange, right?

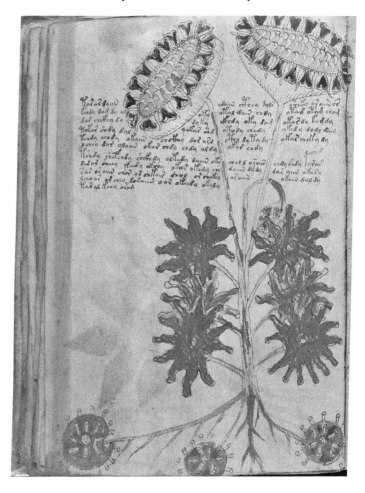

Moving on, we find cosmological medallions, like magical maps, and pharmaceutical drawings of over 100 medicinal herbs. And lastly, there are pages of text, possibly recipes, with star-like flowers marking each entry. Talk about a magical cookbook!

Now, here's the twist in the tale! A history researcher named Nicholas Gibbs thinks he's cracked the code. He believes the

Voynich Manuscript is a guide to women's health, filled with advice stolen from other guides of the time. But hey, the mystery isn't over—the origin, language, and date of the manuscript are still up for debate!

So, young adventurers, the Voynich Manuscript is like a riddle wrapped in mystery, waiting for someone brave enough to unlock its secrets. Who knows what magical discoveries await those who dare to dive into its pages? Keep your eyes wide open, and maybe one day, you'll be the hero who unravels the mysteries of this ancient enchanted book.

Attempting to Decipher Languages and Symbols

After its discovery, scholars from different fields tried their hand at deciphering its mysterious contents. Imagine being a detective in a world of ancient puzzles!

In the early 1900s, a person named William Newbold thought a friar from the 1200s wrote the Voynich Manuscript as a scientific guide, using tiny symbols seen only with a micro-scope. It's a genius idea, right? But, sadly, another person named John Manly, who was a literature professor and code-breaker, proved that Newbold's methods were more like guesses than real science.

Now, meet William and Elizebeth Friedman, a super-smart codebreaking duo. During World War I, they used manual calculations on the Voynich Manuscript, but later on, IBM machines made their code-cracking work faster. Even the National Security Agency got involved in the 1950s, using the manuscript to show off their cool computer skills without revealing secret spy messages.

As technology advanced, so did the tools used to decipher the Voynich Manuscript. Today, researchers like Lisa Fagin Davis use sophisticated computer analysis to critique proposed solutions. It's like having a magical magnifying glass to examine every nook and cranny of the mysterious book.

But the real magic lies in the variety of theories brought forward. Botanist Arthur Tucker believed the plants depicted were from the 16th-century Americas, while others argued over the manuscript's randomness or meaningful language. It's like a battle of wizards using computers, statistics, and even a dash of good old-fashioned guessing.

In 2017, Nicholas Gibbs, our daring history researcher, claimed to have cracked the code, declaring the manuscript a medieval health manual. However, fellow adventurers quickly challenged his findings, arguing that other experts had beaten him to the punch. It seems the mystery remains unbroken, and the quest for understanding continues.

Even in Canada, a duo claimed success in deciphering parts of the manuscript using a computer program. Their algorithm, like a digital spell book, turned the text into vowelless alphagrams, revealing possible Hebrew words. But, alas, Google Translate couldn't quite make sense of it all. Talk about a tricky language puzzle!

Theories about the manuscript's true meaning vary—from gibberish sold by secret philosophers to a pidgin prayer book from a heretical Christian sect. Scholars remain divided, and the Voynich Manuscript continues to resist being fully understood, much like a magical spell that won't reveal its secrets.

So, young adventurers, the quest to unlock the mysteries of the Voynich Manuscript marches on. Will it ever surrender its secrets, or will it remain an enigma for generations to come? Only time will tell!

Theories About Its Origin: From Practical to Outlandish

The manuscript had quite the journey through history. Discovered in 1912 by a book dealer named Wilfrid Voynich, it now lives in a special library at Yale University. Some folks thought it might be the work of a smart guy named Roger Bacon in the 1200s, while others believed it could be a Tudor prank by astrologer John Dee and his friend Edward Kelley. But guess what? Science decided to be a buzzkill in 2009 when radiocarbon dating revealed that the manuscript was actually from the 15th century, way before the Tudor era.

Now, let's talk about some intriguing details in the drawings. There's a tiny castle with special crenelations (those pointy notches on the top of castles), suggesting it might be linked to Northern Italy, especially the Scaliger family from around Verona. Another clue comes from the zodiac section, where Sagittarius, usually shown as a centaur, is a human with a crossbow. Similar drawings popped up in German manuscripts from the 1400s to 1500s.

A historian named Sergio Toresella thinks the herbal drawings in the manuscript have a style from Northern Italy around 1460. He sees a mix of Italian and German influences, making the origin of the Voynich Manuscript a bit like an "Alpine" mystery. Imagine it as a treasure hunt where the clues are hidden in the drawings and writing styles, leading us through the enchanted lands of medieval Europe.

So, young detectives, the quest to uncover the origin of the Voynich Manuscript is like putting together pieces of a magical puzzle. It might have connections to Italy, Germany, or maybe both!

Why It Continues to Intrigue: The Unbroken Code

This 600-year-old puzzle, a mysterious medieval book with around 240 pages, written in a language no one can understand, is like a treasure map guarded by mythical creatures. Despite its mysterious nature, countless brave researchers have tried to crack its secrets over the years. Everyone dreams of being the hero who proves their smarts and unlocks the hidden knowledge within.

Alas, the Voynich Manuscript is like a challenging game where hardly anyone understands all the different rules and clues. Yet researchers find joy not just in solving the mystery but in the journey itself. In the past five years, experts in computational linguistics, physics, computer science, and cryptology have published papers about the Voynich Manuscript, each proposing a unique approach to analyzing the text. Some claims get debunked, but many contribute new tools and ideas to the scientific toolbox.

But here's the thing: The manuscript might be an unsolvable mystery. Imagine it as a language that's so foreign, it's like trying to decipher a secret code. Robert Richards, a historian of science, compares the Voynich text to the language aliens might use—so different from ours that we can't even be sure it's a language at all (Foley, 2020). It's like a puzzle piece from a different dimension!

So, dear adventurers, the Voynich Manuscript might remain an enigma, a medieval joke that we just can't get. Maybe the magic lies not just in finding the solution but in the wonder and excitement of the quest itself. Who knows what mysteries the manuscript still holds, waiting to be uncovered by the brave hearts and sharp minds of future explorers?

Chapter 9
The Amber Room

Once upon a time, in the enchanted realm of art and history, there was a spellbinding masterpiece known as the Amber Room, a brilliant treasure once termed the "Eighth Wonder of the World." Allow me to take you on an adventure through the interesting history and strange disappearance of this valuable piece!

Our story begins in the early 18th century, when the skillful hands of Andreas Schlüter, a German artist and architect, created the Amber Room for Charlottenburg Palace. However, fate had other intentions, and the room ended up in the Berlin City Palace, where it caught the attention of Russia's powerful Peter the Great during a state visit in 1716.

To solidify the bond between Russia and Prussia, Frederick William I generously gifted the Amber Room to the Russian Empire. The room, adorned with over six tons of amber, transformed into a magical wonderland. It became the crown jewel of Catherine Palace in Pushkin, just outside St. Petersburg, enchanting visitors for years.

However, when the shadows of World War II fell, the Amber Room faced an uncertain future. The Nazis, led by the infamous Adolf Hitler, staged a massive art theft, stealing treasures from around Europe. Among their riches was the invaluable Amber Room.

The Disappearance in World War II: A Mystery Unfolds

As the war dragged on, the Nazis decided to relocate their stolen goods to safer locations. The Amber Room, once a symbol of beauty and brotherhood, was now challenged with the horrors of war. The Royal Air Force bombed its temporary home, Königsberg, in 1944, wreaking disaster, and the oncoming Red Army caused much more devastation in 1945.

The destiny of the Amber Room got obscured by mystery. Some believed it met its end in the fiery chaos, while others clung to the hope that it might still be hidden, waiting to be discovered.

Decades later, declassified documents from the Russian National Archives added a layer to the mystery. Alexander Brusov, a tenacious investigator, suggested that the Amber Room likely perished amid the devastation in Königsberg. His report spoke of damaged and burnt fragments found in the castle's cellar.

Yet, the enigma persisted, with whispers of Soviet secrets. Was it a Cold War charade, blaming the Nazis to hide their own role in the tragedy? Or were they earnestly searching for answers within their own ranks?

And so, the legend of the Amber Room continues—a spellbinding tale of art, war, and the relentless quest for truth. The Eighth Wonder of the World may be lost in the folds of time, but its story lives on, captivating hearts and sparking imagination in those who dare to explore its mysterious history.

The Hunt for the Lost Treasure: Searches and Claims

Tales of unconfirmed sightings and mysterious recoveries have added layers of intrigue to this captivating story. Some claimed to have witnessed the Amber Room being loaded onto the *Wilhelm Gustloff* in 1945, which tragically met its end when it was torpedoed and sunk by a Soviet submarine. Despite several explorations of the wreckage, no tangible evidence has surfaced to confirm that the Amber Room was ever on board. It's like a puzzle missing its crucial piece, leaving us to wonder if the treasure lies hidden beneath the waves.

In 1997, a twist in the tale occurred when parts of the fourth Florentine mosaic from the Amber Room were discovered in the possession of the son of a German soldier. The soldier claimed to have stolen it during the room's removal in 1941 or 1945. This revelation added a new layer of mystery—fragments of the Amber Room resurfacing after decades of silence.

These contradictory events have fueled numerous theories about the Amber Room's fate. Was it truly lost in the chaos of war, or does it lie hidden, waiting to be rediscovered? The treasure hunt continues, but all investigations have hit dead ends, leaving the fate of the Amber Room shrouded in uncertainty.

The most likely explanation suggests that it met its demise in the bombings of Königsberg, or perhaps remnants still lie concealed beneath the castle in a secret vault. However, the plot thickens. In 1968, Soviet leader Leonid Brezhnev ordered the destruction of Königsberg Castle, making it nearly impossible to conduct on-site research at the last known resting place of the Amber Room. The truth seemed further out of reach.

Replicas and Remembrance: Keeping the Legend Alive

As the years rolled on, the Amber Room continued to cast its enchanting spell, becoming an obsession for some brave souls who dared to embark on its mysterious quest. Meet Georg Stein, a former German soldier and history enthusiast who dedicated much of his life to uncovering the secrets of the Amber Room. Yet, in a tragic turn of events, his journey took a dark twist, ending in his untimely demise in a Bavarian forest in 1987. The circumstances were as mysterious as the room itself—Georg was found murdered, his life cut short with a scalpel.

Similarly, General Yuri Gusev, deputy head of Russia's foreign intelligence unit, found himself entangled in the Amber Room's web. His mysterious death in a car accident in 1992 added another layer of intrigue. Rumors circulated that he may have been the source for a journalist investigating the Amber Room's whereabouts. The quest for this lost treasure seemed to exact a toll on those who dared to pursue it.

Yet, as hope flickered that the Amber Room might be found, a new chapter emerged. In 1979, the former USSR decided to breathe life back into the legend. With only a single box of relics from the room and 86 black-and-white photos taken just before World War II, craftsmen embarked on a 23-year journey to reconstruct the Amber Room. The spark of creativity, fueled by remnants of the past, aimed to resurrect the magic of this ancient masterpiece.

Today, the recreated Amber Room stands proudly at Catherine Palace in the Tsarskoye Selo State Museum and Heritage Site in St. Petersburg. Imagine walking into a room where the walls glow with the warmth of orange and gold, bringing the ancient allure of fossilized resin back to life. The recreated treasure, a testament to determination and the enduring power of art, captures the hearts and imaginations of those who stand in its presence.

As the legend lives on, the Amber Room continues to weave its tale of mystery and remembrance. Its recreated beauty beckons, a beacon of history that sparks curiosity and wonder in the hearts of those who dare to explore its captivating story. The lost treasure may remain a puzzle, but the recreated masterpiece stands as a living testament to the magic that can arise from the echoes of the past.

Chapter 10
Jack the Ripper

Once upon a time, in the bustling streets of London, there lived a mysterious figure known as Jack the Ripper. This mysterious character made history by doing something really strange and scary. Imagine this: Five ladies were murdered, and their bodies were changed in an unusual way, like a puzzle only someone with special knowledge about the human body could solve. The strange part? Nobody ever caught or even saw Jack the Ripper, making this person one of the most infamous criminals in England and the whole wide world.

The spooky events all happened in a small area called Whitechapel, in London's East End. It was like a mystery game, but with real consequences. From August 7th to September 10th of 1888, within just a month, five terrifying incidents took place, all within a mile of each other! It's almost like Jack the Ripper had a secret map leading to these unfortunate events.

Now, Jack the Ripper had another creepy nickname: "Leather Apron." Picture someone wearing a leather apron doing something scary in the dark corners of the city.

But here's where it gets even more mysterious: letters. Yes, letters! Jack the Ripper supposedly sent chilling letters to the police, bragging about the scary things done and making predictions about more mysteries to come. The police, known as Scotland Yard, were the detectives trying to solve the case. And guess what? The name "Jack the Ripper" actually came from one of these letters. Some folks think it might have been a trick, a hoax, like magic smoke and mirrors to keep everyone on their toes.

Despite lots and lots of clever people trying to find out who Jack the Ripper really was, the mystery remains unsolved. Nobody knows the name or the reason behind these scary actions. It's like the world's biggest puzzle, and the pieces are hiding in the shadows of history.

So, the mystery of Jack the Ripper still lingers in the air, like a ghost story waiting to be solved. Maybe one day, a brave detective or historian will uncover the secrets of this mysterious figure, and the story of Jack the Ripper will finally be put to rest. Until then, let the mystery live on in the pages of history, waiting for someone to unveil the truth behind the chilling tale.

The Ripper's Reign: A Look at the Murders

The story begins between April of 1888 and February of 1891, with a total of 11 women meeting a tragic end in the East End of London. The police gathered information about these heartbreaking events in a file called "The Whitechapel Murders." Out of these, five women are believed to be the work of Jack the Ripper, the mysterious figure who left his mark on history with a taunting letter sent to the Central News Office in 1888.

These five women, known as the "Canonical Five," faced their unfortunate fate between the 31st of August and the 9th of November in 1888. Imagine a dark and foggy London night, where whispers of mystery filled the air, and the unknown lurked in the shadows. Below were some of the noteworthy victims during the Ripper's reign.

1. **Emma Smith (April 3rd, 1888):** Imagine a quiet morning, and Emma Smith walking through the eerie streets. She survived a frightening attack, managing to reach the London Hospital, where she shared her horrifying tale of being attacked by a gang of youths. Her courage echoes through time, a survivor in the

face of danger. But her story begins a series of dark events in East London.

2. **Martha Tabram (August 8th, 1888):** Martha's story is one of debate. Her life ended tragically on a first-floor landing, and people wonder if she was a victim of Jack the Ripper. She had met a soldier on Whitechapel High Street, venturing into George Yard with him. The mystery deepens with Martha's fate.

3. **Mary Nichols (August 31st, 1888):** The chilling saga started to feel real with Mary Nichols found in Bucks Row, now Durward Street. She is considered the first official victim of Jack the Ripper. Picture a gateway shrouded in darkness, and a tragic fate that set the stage for the horror to come.

4. **Annie Chapman (September 8th, 1888):** The unease in the area turned into outright panic with Annie Chapman's murder in the backyard of number 29 Hanbury Street. A turning point in the tale, the residents now faced the terrifying reality of a serial killer in their midst.

5. **Elizabeth Stride (September 30th, 1888):** The "night of the double event" saw the first victim, Elizabeth Stride, meeting a mysterious end. It seems the killer was interrupted, adding another layer of mystery to the chilling narrative.

6. **Catherine Eddowes (September 30th, 1888):** The same night, the second victim, Catherine Eddowes, faced a gruesome fate in Mitre Square. The killer took away a trophy, leaving the residents horrified and wondering when the nightmare would end.

7. **Mary Kelly (November 9th, 1888):** Just when they thought it was over, Jack the Ripper returned, claiming the life of Mary Kelly in her room in

Miller's Court. The horror continued, leaving the district in shock and sorrow.

8. **Alice McKenzie (July 17th, 1889):** After months of silence, fear returned with the discovery of Alice McKenzie's body in Castle Alley. Although experts debate whether she was a victim of Jack the Ripper, the fear of his return lingered in the air.

9. **Frances Coles (November 13th, 1891):** As the year 1891 unfolded, Frances Coles became the last victim in the official Whitechapel Murders file. Arrests were made, and some believed Jack the Ripper had finally been caught. The district sighed in relief, hoping for an end to the nightmare.

The days and weeks that followed saw a return to some semblance of normality, but the memory of these tragic events lingered. The legacy of the crimes focused attention on the plight of the poor in an area later known as "The Abyss." However, whether these murders brought about change to the social conditions remains a mystery, much like the identity of Jack the Ripper himself. The puzzle continues, and the pages of history whisper the tales of those who once walked the darkened streets of Whitechapel.

Who Was Jack the Ripper? - Suspects and Theories

The identity of this elusive figure remains shrouded in darkness, with over a hundred names tossed into the swirling fog of speculation. Some suspects seem plausible, while others are downright absurd, making the search for Jack the Ripper akin to navigating a maze of shadows.

Each passing year brings forth new books claiming to have cracked the case, adding fresh perspectives to the world's greatest murder mystery. Some authors uncover intriguing details, like precious puzzle pieces, but most tend to bend the facts to fit their theories rather than objectively examining the evidence.

In the early days, the police focused their investigations on local gangs, known as "High-Rip" gangs, suspecting they might be behind the gruesome crimes. However, as the panic and publicity intensified, the police shifted their attention. By September of 1888, they leaned toward the idea of a lone assassin. Speculation arose that the killer possessed medical or anatomical knowledge, prompting inquiries into medical students with asylum experience. Yet this lead turned out to be a dead end, as the movements of these students were accounted for, eliminating them as suspects.

Diverging opinions emerged regarding the killer's skill level. Some believed he demonstrated medical expertise, while others argued his abilities were no more than those of a butcher or slaughterman. Extensive investigations were conducted among local butchers and slaughterhouses, but alibis checked out, leaving the police empty-handed.

The Victorian police tirelessly conducted over 2,000 interviews, investigated over 300 individuals, and detained 80 people in their quest to unmask Jack the Ripper. Despite their efforts, no concrete evidence pointed toward a specific suspect living in the district. The fog of uncertainty persisted, and the true identity of Jack the Ripper remained elusive.

As the curtain fell on the Jack the Ripper murders, a parade of suspects emerged. Some were outlandish, like Prince Albert Edward Victor, Lewis Carroll, the Freemasons, and even Dr. Barnardo. Others, such as Thomas Cutbush and Carl Feigenbaum, were initially discarded but resurfaced as potential culprits through modern research or the opening of asylum records.

The mystery deepens with each passing revelation, and the enigma of Jack the Ripper continues to captivate the imagination of those seeking to unveil the face behind the shadows. The truth remains elusive, and the pages of history are filled with countless names, each a potential key to unlocking the mystery that still echoes through the cobblestone streets of Victorian London.

The Ripper's Legacy - Impact on Crime Investigation

Today, people worldwide visit the memorials of Jack the Ripper's victims, laying flowers and trinkets in remembrance. Mary Nichols, Annie Chapman, Elizabeth Stride, Catherine Eddowes, and Mary Kelly, once forgotten, now symbolize hardship and tragedy.

As we reflect on their lives, a paradox emerges. These names might have faded away were it not for the unknown assailant, Jack the Ripper. In the quiet moments by the memorials, we confront not only their gruesome deaths but also the harsh realities of their existence, shedding light on the struggles in Victorian Whitechapel.

The legacy of Jack the Ripper becomes a testament to memory's resilience. Though the infamous figure's identity remains unknown, the victims' stories endure, inviting us to ponder life's fragility and the power of remembrance. Our journey through history concludes with the shadows of the past still whispering their tales to those who listen.

Chapter 11
The Loch Ness Monster

There exists a magnificent lake called Loch Ness amid Scotland's lovely countryside. But this isn't just any lake; it is home to a legendary beast, a mysterious being that has inspired legends for millennia.

Let's go back in time to the sixth century, when a wise man named Saint Columba visited the Highlands. His writings told of a peculiar encounter with a "water beast" dragging a poor soul beneath the waves. This marked the first mention of the creature we now fondly call Nessie.

Now, zip ahead to the year 1933, where Aldie Mackay, managing the Drumnadrochit Hotel, had an astonishing sighting. She spoke of seeing "an enormous creature with the body of a whale rolling in the water." And just like that, Nessie became a riddle of modern times.

People began spotting Nessie more frequently, describing her as a creature with a lengthy neck and flippers, much like a dinosaur called a plesiosaur. They even estimated the size of her humps—the largest one measured longer than a really big boat!

Over the years, more than a thousand Nessie sightings were recorded. Some were in photographs, like the famous "Surgeon's Photograph" in 1934, while others were folks sharing their amazing stories. A man named George Edwards even boasted of having the "most convincing Nessie photograph ever."

Here's the tricky part. Some of these sightings turned out to be tricks, people playing pretend with Nessie. But others remained a puzzle, leaving us wondering whether Nessie is real or just a figment of imagination.

So, the Loch Ness mystery and its mythical monster continue to captivate people of all ages. As you tour the stunning Scottish scenery and stare at the shimmering waters of Loch Ness, keep an eye out for Nessie, the elusive and magical creature of the deep!

Searching for Nessie: Expeditions and Evidence

As folks all around the globe kept getting fascinated by the Loch Ness mystery, some really brave adventurers and scientists decided to go on cool expeditions. They wanted to find out what's really going on beneath the waves of Loch Ness.

Back in the 1960s, British universities sent out special missions equipped with sonar gadgets—those are tools that can figure out if something's moving underwater. Even though they didn't actually find a Loch Ness monster, the people using the sonar did pick up some big, mysterious things moving below the water's surface. Now, imagine how excited everyone must have been!

Fast forward to 1975, and another group of explorers had an even fancier setup. They used both sonar and underwater cameras to peek at Nessie. And guess what happened? They snapped a photo that looked like a giant flipper, similar to what you'd see on a whale or dolphin. They tweaked the photo to make it clearer, and suddenly, Loch Ness felt even more magical.

But, like in any good mystery tale, things weren't as straightforward as they seemed. Some photos claiming to show Nessie turned out to be fake—like that famous one from 1934. It was revealed that the creature in that photo was just a plastic-and-wooden head stuck to a toy submarine. Can you believe it?

Even in the 1980s and 1990s, more expeditions with sonar readings didn't quite settle the question of whether Nessie was real. Then in 2018, scientists took on a mission to study Loch Ness' DNA, hoping to find out who lives there. They did find lots of eels, but no signs of a plesiosaur or a huge sea monster. Some folks even started thinking maybe Nessie is just a really big eel after all!

Even though we don't have rock-solid proof that Nessie is out there, the Loch Ness Monster has become a magical part of Scotland's tale. People from all over visit Loch Ness, and the mystery has even helped Scotland make nearly $80 million every year. So, whether Nessie is real or not, she's turned Loch Ness into a place full of wonder and adventure!

Debating Existence: Science vs. Myth

Even in modern times, more than a thousand people claim to have glimpsed Nessie, the friendly nickname given to the creature by the locals. However, there's a twist: Everyone seems to describe Nessie a bit differently. Some say she looks like a salamander; others compare her to a whale; and some even think she might be a giant seal! Imagine that!

But here's the curious part: Most of the time, the weather and visibility weren't great when people reported seeing Nessie. And, interestingly, many of these witnesses already knew the legend of Loch Ness, the home of the famous monster. Could this knowledge have influenced what they thought they saw?

Now, let's talk about evidence. Finding real proof of Nessie's existence is like solving a puzzle. No one has ever captured her, taken a super-clear photo, or had a biologist examine her up close. Some people argue that if Nessie were a large creature like a dinosaur, she would have to come up to the surface often. Many courageous people, including scuba divers and sonar specialists, have explored the dark waters of Loch Ness but have found no trace of Nessie. In 2019, experts examined

DNA samples from the lake, and guess what? They discovered no trace of a dinosaur or a gigantic reptile (Little, 2023).

Here's another intriguing fact: Loch Ness has only existed for around 10,000 years, following the last glacial era on Earth. But dinosaurs, those magnificent animals from long ago, vanished around 65 million years ago. So it's not likely that an ancient aquatic dinosaur existed in Loch Ness.

Moreover, for Nessie to be real and stick around for so long, there would need to be more of her kind—a whole family, perhaps! Animals usually don't live for hundreds of years, as the legend suggests. They live their lives and leave the stage for the next generation.

So, young adventurers, as you ponder the mystery of Nessie, remember that legends can be magical, but finding the truth requires a sprinkle of scientific curiosity and a dash of critical thinking! The Loch Ness Monster continues to be a captivating tale, whether she's a mythical wonder or a creature still waiting to reveal herself.

Nessie in Popular Culture: Books, Movies, and Tourism

The Loch Ness Monster has created her own wonderful universe and is now more than just a real-life mystery—she has appeared in literature and movies! Despite being referred to as a "monster," Nessie is usually portrayed as a friendly giant in the myths. Imagine a friendly and wonderful creature swimming joyfully in the deep waters of Loch Ness! Nessie stars in films such as *Loch Ness* and *Happy Ness: The Secret of the Loch* from 1996, and she isn't terrifying at all.

Instead, she is a likable creature who makes friends with everyone she encounters.

Now, every good story needs a bit of excitement, right? In some rare tales, Nessie is shown as a bit of a threat. In the 1981 film *The Loch Ness Horror* and the 2008 film *Loch Ness Terror* (also known as *Beyond Loch Ness*), the monster is portrayed as something to be feared. Picture Nessie as a mysterious and powerful force causing a bit of chaos!

But hold on, there's more! Not every Nessie fits neatly into the "friendly" or "threatening" categories. In the movie *7 Faces of Dr. Lao*, the Loch Ness Monster is presented in a unique way. In this magical tale, Nessie starts as a tiny fish and magically transforms into the familiar serpentine shape when out of the water. Even though she looks big and impressive, she remains harmless and enchanting.

Nessie is more than just a movie star; she also appears in novels, cartoons, and even T-shirts and posters! People all throughout the world appreciate the Loch Ness Monster in unique ways, making her a symbol of mystery and wonder.

So, as you continue your journey through Loch Ness folklore, remember that Nessie is more than just a creature in the water; she is a fabled figure that has captured people's hearts and imaginations all across the world! Whether she's a friendly giant or a strange mystery, Nessie continues to make an impression in the great world of pop culture. Keep your eyes wide open, and who knows? You might spot Nessie in the most unexpected places!

Conclusion

As we walked through the corridors of time, seeking the fascinating places of history's greatest unsolved mysteries, we found ourselves poised on the edge of the unknown. Even with all of today's cutting-edge technology and scientific advances, these mysteries remain unresolved and buried in the shadows of time. It's like a wild frontier where the past whispers secrets, keeping us on our toes.

In an age of quick information and modern devices, the mysteries of the Atlantic, Loch Ness Monster, and Stonehenge keep us captivated. The mysteries of the Amber Room, Bermuda Triangle, and Voynich Manuscript have us scratching our brains, wondering what's going on.

The myths of Jack the Ripper, the Turin Shroud, and the lost Roanoke Colony reveal that humans have long enjoyed latching on to stories that stretch beyond reality. Those mysterious stories have a way of sparking our interest, making us dig deeper and question the stories passed down through time.

Conclusion

In this vast land of things we don't know, there's something cool about the beauty of the unknown. It's like a blank canvas where our imaginative minds may run wild with possibilities. These mysteries aren't just mysteries waiting to be solved; they're portals to a world where curiosity is the key to making new discoveries.

To you youngsters, who are about to embark on your own adventures, these unresolved riddles are more than just puzzles to solve. They're invitations to explore, question, and be amazed at the stuff we haven't figured out yet. Embrace the mystery because, in a world where knowing stuff is cool, the questions left hanging are what fuel our never-ending curiosity.

So, as you dive into your own history adventures, remember that the unknown isn't something to be scared of—it's the spark that keeps us looking for answers. May your curiosity lead you to awesome discoveries and thrilling adventures,

Conclusion

because in chasing the unknown, the best stories are waiting
to be written.

References

Mega Luxury. (2023, May 20). *Fascinating filthy secrets of ancient egyptian pharaohs.* YouTube. https://www.youtube.com/watch?v=_e-J4dx0zgjg&ab_channel=MegaLuxury

Atlantis: Symbols, legends, and modern interpretations. (2023, August 5). Kalisma Bijoux. https://kalismabijoux.com/en/blog/amulets/atlantis-unveiling-the-enigma-and-its-symbolism

Augustyn, A. (2018). Bermuda Triangle. In *Encyclopædia Britannica.* https://www.britannica.com/place/Bermuda-Triangle

Bad Things: True Crime. (2023). The lost city of Atlantis: What most likely happened [Website Video]. In *YouTube.* https://www.youtube.com/watch?v=_nVmiK_WB4s&ab_channel=BadThings%3ATrueCrime

Ballan, D. (2023, November 22). *Unraveling the enigma of the shroud of Turin: Between faith and science.* English plus Podcast. https://english-pluspodcast.com/unraveling-the-enigma-of-the-shroud-of-turin-between-faith-and-science/#:~:text=For%20skeptics%20and%20scien-tists%2C%20it

BBC - history - historic figures: Jack the ripper (?). (2014). Www.bbc.co.uk. https://www.bbc.co.uk/history/historic_figures/ripper_jack_the.shtml

Benzine, V. (2022, September 22). *One great mystery of the pyramids' construction has been solved. it involves boats.* Artnet News. https://news.artnet.com/art-world/pyramids-discovery-khufu-branch-2179716

Bermuda and its Triangle – fact and fictions. (2017, February 8). Saga. https://www.saga.co.uk/magazine/travel/destinations/caribbean/bermuda-and-its-triangle-fact-and-fictions

Blakemore, E. (2023, April 20). *Why the myth of Atlantis just won't die.* National Geographic. https://www.nationalgeographic.co.uk/history-and-civilisation/2023/04/why-the-myth-of-atlantis-just-wont-die

Cascone, S. (2020, November 6). *Archaeologists may have finally solved the mystery of the disappearance of Roanoke's lost colony.* Artnet News. https://news.artnet.com/art-world/archaeologists-mystery-lost-roanoke-lost-colony-1921594

Chapman, A., & Henbest, N. (2022, February 8). *Was Stonehenge used for astronomy?* Sky at Night Magazine. https://www.skyatnightmagazine.com/space-science/stonehenge-astronomy

References

Chohu, S. K. (2023, August 9). *The mysterious tale of the lost city of Atlantis.* Geeks. https://vocal.media/geeks/the-mysterious-tale-of-the-lost-city-of-atlantis

Colossal Cranium. (2019). The "lost" city of Atlantis | Colossal Mysteries [Website Video]. In *YouTube.* https://www.youtube.com/watch?v=fVjD-BXOjLx0&ab_channel=ColossalCranium

Cook, C. (2022, August 4). *3 mysteries archaeologists still haven't figured out about ancient Egypt's pyramids.* Matador Network. https://matador-network.com/read/pyramid-mysteries/

Cornish, P. (2021, November 24). *Stonehenge's four biggest mysteries - the unsolved questions.* Express. https://www.express.co.uk/news/science/1526517/Stonehenge-biggest-mysteries-why-built-stones-evg

Crookes, D., & All About Space magazine. (2020, July 8). *South Atlantic anomaly: Have astronomers finally explained space's Bermuda Triangle?* Space. https://www.space.com/bermuda-triangle-in-space.html

Crowe, F. (2022). The Voynich manuscript: Decoded. *Journal of Historical Archaeology & Anthropological Sciences*, *7*(3), 94–131. https://doi.org/10.15406/jhaas.2022.07.00262

Drye, W. (2017, January 21). *Explaining the legend of Atlantis.* History; National Geographic. https://www.nationalgeographic.com/history/article/atlantis

Egyptian pyramids - facts, use & construction. (2009, October 14). History. https://www.history.com/topics/ancient-egypt/the-egyptian-pyramids#section_4

Fanti, G. (2019). Science and christian faith: The example of the Turin shroud. *Global Journal of Archaeology & Anthropology*, *8*(1), 1–7. https://doi.org/10.19080/GJAA.2018.07.555726

Fascination with Bermuda Triangle persists, 60 years later. (2005, December 5). NPR. https://www.npr.org/templates/story/story.php?storyId=5038874

Five of the most mysterious Bermuda Triangle disappearances. (2022, January 12). Sky HISTORY TV Channel. https://www.history.co.uk/articles/five-of-the-most-mysterious-bermuda-triangle-disappearances

Foley, J. (2020, February 12). *The strange quest to crack the Voynich code.* Undark Magazine. https://undark.org/2020/02/12/decoding-bizarre-voynich-manuscript/

Giller, G. (2020, July 21). *Where is the lost city of Atlantis — and does it even exist?* Discover Magazine. https://www.discovermagazine.com/planet-earth/where-is-the-lost-city-of-atlantis-and-does-it-even-exist

Golomb, J. (2010, November 8). *Why the Nasca lines are among Peru's greatest mysteries.* National Geographic. https://www.nationalgeographic.com/history/article/nasca-lines

References

Handwerk, B. (2017, January 21). *Pyramids of Giza*. National Geographic. https://www.nationalgeographic.com/history/article/giza-pyramids

Hogeback, J. (2019). The lost colony of Roanoke. In *Encyclopædia Britannica*. https://www.britannica.com/story/the-lost-colony-of-roanoke

How the nazca lines were made. (2018, March 7). Peru Travel Blog | Machu Travel Peru. https://www.machutravelperu.com/blog/how-were-the-nazca-lines-made

Ibrahim, N. (2022, October 13). *What does the mysterious Voynich manuscript really say?* Snopes. https://www.snopes.com/articles/460139/voynich-manuscript/

Illsley, C. L. (2020, October 19). *The lost city of Atlantis*. WorldAtlas. https://www.worldatlas.com/articles/the-lost-city-of-atlantis.html

Is the Loch Ness monster real? (2020, January 16). Scottish Tours. https://www.scottishtours.co.uk/blog/is-the-loch-ness-monster-real/

Jack the Ripper. (2010, November 8). HISTORY; A&E Television Networks. https://www.history.com/topics/european-history/jack-the-ripper

Jack the ripper suspects. (2019, January 31). JackTheRipper. https://thejack-therippertour.com/casebook/suspects/

Jack the ripper victims. (2019, March 8). JackTheRipper. https://thejack-therippertour.com/casebook/victims/

Jarus, O. (2012, August 14). *Nazca Lines: Mysterious geoglyphs in Peru*. Live Science. https://www.livescience.com/22370-nazca-lines.html

Jarus, O. (2021, November 20). *What happened to the "vanished" colonists at Roanoke?* Live Science. https://www.livescience.com/vanished-colonists-at-roanoke

Jones, R. (2010, December 31). *The jack the ripper suspects*. Jack the Ripper. https://www.jack-the-ripper.org/suspects.htm

Jones, R. (2020). *Attack on Ada Wilson - newspaper reports*. Jack the Ripper. https://www.jack-the-ripper.org/victims-of-jack-the-ripper.htm

Jones, R. (2021, April 8). *Jack the ripper - history, victims, letters, suspects*. Jack the Ripper; Richard Jones. https://www.jack-the-ripper.org/

Jones, R. (2023, February 3). *Jack the ripper tour*. Jack-The-Ripper-Tour.com. https://www.jack-the-ripper-tour.com/the-victims/

Kannan, A. M. (2023). *The secret of the pharaoh's tomb: Unraveling the mysteries of ancient egypt*. Fiction. https://vocal.media/fiction/the-secret-of-the-pharaoh-s-tomb-unraveling-the-mysteries-of-ancient-egypt

Kozak, C. (2023, June 9). *Artifacts appear to confirm "first contact" at Roanoke Island*. Coastal Review. https://coastalreview.org/2023/06/artifacts-appear-to-confirm-first-contact-at-roanoke-island/

Legend of the Loch Ness monster. (2015a, March 28). Loch Ness by Jacobite. https://www.jacobite.co.uk/loch-ness-monster

References

Legend of the Loch Ness monster. (2015b, March 28). Loch Ness by Jacobite. https://www.jacobite.co.uk/loch-ness-monster

Little, B. (2020, April 9). *The Shroud of Turin: 7 Intriguing Facts*. HISTORY. https://www.history.com/news/shroud-turin-facts

Little, M. A. (2023, February 27). *Is the Loch Ness monster real?* The Conversation. https://theconversation.com/is-the-loch-ness-monster-real-197338

Loch Ness Monster sighted. (2019, February 21). HISTORY. https://www.history.com/this-day-in-history/loch-ness-monster-sighted

Loch Ness monster sighted. (2023, August 22). National Geographic - Education. https://education.nationalgeographic.org/resource/loch-ness-monster-sighted/

Mambra, S. (2017, October 9). *Top 10 amazing facts about the lost city of Atlantis*. Marine Insight. https://www.marineinsight.com/maritime-history/top-10-amazing-facts-about-the-lost-city-of-atlantis/

Mambra, S. (2019, February 26). *5 famous mysterious stories of the Bermuda Triangle*. Marine Insight. https://www.marineinsight.com/maritime-history/5-famous-mysterious-stories-of-the-bermuda-triangle

Miller, N. (2023, September 18). *The lost settlers: Delving into the mystery of the Roanoke Colony*. Discovery UK. https://www.discoveryuk.com/mysteries/the-lost-settlers-delving-into-the-mystery-of-the-roanoke-colony/

Milligan, M. (2022, January 6). *The mystery of the missing Amber Room*. HeritageDaily - Archaeology News. https://www.heritagedaily.com/2022/01/the-mystery-of-the-missing-amber-room/142423

Misachi , J. (2017, February 27). *Mysteries of egypt: The curse of the pharaohs*. WorldAtlas. https://www.worldatlas.com/articles/mysteries-of-egypt-the-curse-of-the-pharaohs.html

Mizen, S. (2020, June 2). *The Voynich Manuscript: who wrote the mystery medieval codex and what is it trying to tell us?* HistoryExtra. https://www.historyextra.com/period/medieval/what-is-the-voynich-manuscript-voynich-code-decoded-who-was-voynich/

Muir, J. K. (2014, November 17). *Five pop culture memories of the Bermuda Triangle craze of the 1970s*. Flashbak. https://flashbak.com/five-pop-culture-memories-of-the-bermuda-triangle-craze-of-the-1970s-25668/

Newitz, A. (2017, September 8). *The mysterious Voynich manuscript has finally been decoded*. Ars Technica. https://arstechnica.com/science/2017/09/the-mysterious-voynich-manuscript-has-finally-been-decoded/

Novak, S. (2022, July 26). *Stonehenge may be an ancient solar calendar*. Astronomy Magazine. https://www.astronomy.com/science/stonehenge-may-be-an-ancient-solar-calendar/

References

Onion, A., Sullivan, M., Mullen, M., & Zapata, C. (2010a, June 1). *Stonehenge*. History. https://www.history.com/topics/european-history/stonehenge#section_3

Onion, A., Sullivan, M., Mullen, M., & Zapata, C. (2010b, October 7). *Bermuda Triangle*. HISTORY. https://www.history.com/topics/folklore/bermuda-triangle#bermuda-triangle-theories-and-counter-theories

Onion, Amanda., Sullivan, M., Mullen, M., & Zapata, C. (2017, December 4). *Nazca Lines*. HISTORY. https://www.history.com/topics/south-america/nazca-lines#section_2

Onion, Amanda., Sullivan, M., Mullen, M., & Zapata, C. (2018, August 21). *Roanoke Colony Deserted*. HISTORY. https://www.history.com/this-day-in-history/roanoke-colony-deserted

Piippo, M. (2020). Loch Ness monster and her impact on culture Loch Ness monster and her impact on culture. In *Inspire*. https://scholarworks.uni.edu/cgi/viewcontent.cgi?article=1073&context=csbsresearchconf

Red History Riddle. (2023, July 20). *The lost city of atlantis: Myth or reality?* Medium. https://medium.com/@redhistorybrainriddle/the-lost-city-of-atlantis-myth-or-reality-b93a44f9e582

Reinhard, J. (1986). *The Nazca lines a new perspective on their origin and meaning*. Lima Ed. Los Pinos.

Rogan, J. (2022, November 6). *Joe Rogan: The secrets & mysteries of the Egyptian pyramids!* The Archaeologist. https://www.thearchaeologist.org/blog/joe-rogan-the-secrets-amp-mysteries-of-the-egyptian-pyramids

Rucker, R. (2022, July 6). The mysteries of the shroud of Turin. *ASNT Pulse*. https://blog.asnt.org/the-mysteries-of-the-shroud-of-turin/

Ruggles, C. (1997). Astronomy and Stonehenge. In *The British Academy* (pp. 203–229). Proceedings of the British Academy. https://www.thebritishacademy.ac.uk/documents/3920/92p203.pdf

Scharping, N. (2021, March 11). The Bermuda Triangle: What science can tell us about the mysterious ocean region. *Discover Magazine*. https://www.discovermagazine.com/planet-earth/the-bermuda-triangle-what-science-can-tell-us-about-the-mysterious-ocean

Sedunova, I. (2021, May 7). *Russia's "eighth wonder of the world."* BBC. https://www.bbc.com/travel/article/20210506-russias-eighth-wonder-of-the-world

Shaw, G. (2020, June 18). *Has Yale's mysterious Voynich manuscript finally been deciphered?* The Art Newspaper - International Art News and Events. https://www.theartnewspaper.com/2020/06/18/has-yales-mysterious-voynich-manuscript-finally-been-deciphered

References

Shroud of Turin. (2023, December 6). Encyclopedia Britannica. https://www.britannica.com/place/Turin-Italy

Shuttleworth, C. (2023, August 27). *The mystery of how Egypt's great pyramids were built has finally been solved*. Indy100. https://www.indy100.com/science-tech/egypt-pyramids-built-mystery-solved-2663989999

Stewart, J. (2018, November 19). *7 surprising facts about the Egyptian pyramids*. My Modern Met. https://mymodernmet.com/egyptian-pyramids/

Stonehenge facts for kids. (2017, September). National Geographic Kids. https://www.natgeokids.com/uk/discover/history/general-history/stonehenge-facts/

Storck, E. N. (2023, April 10). *Secrets of the great pyramids of Giza*. Travel + Leisure. https://www.travelandleisure.com/attractions/secrets-pyramids-giza

The lost city of Atlantis: 4 possible locations. (2015, January 8). The Week. https://theweek.com/articles/486390/lost-city-atlantis-4-possible-locations

The mystery of the Amber Room: the world's greatest lost treasure. (2020, February 26). Sky HISTORY TV Channel. https://www.history.co.uk/article/the-mystery-of-the-amber-room-the-worlds-greatest-lost-treasure

The origin of the Voynich MS. (2022, December 28). Voynich. https://www.voynich.nu/origin.html

The Roanoke Colony (1587–1588). (2021, August 22). Climate in Arts and History. https://www.science.smith.edu/climatelit/the-roanoke-colony/

The shroud of turin website - home page. (2023, December 9). Shroud. https://www.shroud.com/

The shroud of Turin: A convergence of history, faith, and science. (2023, July 21). History Chronicles. https://historychronicles.org/the-shroud-of-turin-a-convergence-of-history-faith-and-science/

The victims of Jack the ripper. (2017, October 25). The History Press. https://www.thehistorypress.co.uk/articles/the-victims-of-jack-the-ripper/

Tikkanen, A. (2018). Loch Ness monster | history, sightings, & facts. In *Encyclopædia Britannica*. https://www.britannica.com/topic/Loch-Ness-monster-legendary-creature

Voynich manuscript. (2018, December 14). Beinecke Rare Book & Manuscript Library; Yale University. https://beinecke.library.yale.edu/collections/highlights/voynich-manuscript

Was Stonehenge built by aliens? (2020, February 17). Britannica. https://www.britannica.com/question/Was-Stonehenge-built-by-aliens

What happened to the "Lost Colony" of Roanoke? (2018, August 23).

References

HISTORY; A&E Television Networks. https://www.history.-com/news/what-happened-to-the-lost-colony-of-roanoke

What is known (and not known) about the Bermuda Triangle. (2018). In *Encyclopædia Britannica*. https://www.britannica.com/story/what-is-known-and-not-known-about-the-bermuda-triangle

What is the Bermuda Triangle? (2010, January 4). NOAA. https://oceanservice.noaa.gov/facts/bermudatri.html

What is the mystery behind the ancient Nazca lines? (2018, December 9). TRT World. https://www.trtworld.com/magazine/what-is-the-mystery-behind-the-ancient-nazca-lines-50318

Who built Stonehenge? (2019). About Stonehenge. https://www.aboutstonehenge.info/who-built-stonehenge/

Why do ships and planes disappear in the Bermuda Triangle? (2023, September 30). *The Times of India*. https://timesofindia.indiatimes.com/etimes/trending/why-do-ships-and-planes-disappear-in-the-bermuda-triangle/articleshow/104042390.cms

Why is Stonehenge important? (2015, March 17). English Heritage. https://www.english-heritage.org.uk/visit/places/stonehenge/history-and-stories/history/significance/

Wikiwand - Loch Ness monster in popular culture. (n.d.). Wikiwand. Retrieved February 6, 2024, from https://www.wikiwand.com/en/Loch_-Ness_Monster_in_popular_culture

Wolfe, B. (2011, April 19). *Roanoke Colonies, The – Encyclopedia Virginia*. Encyclopedia Virginia. https://encyclopediavirginia.org/entries/roanoke-colonies-the/

Worrell, B. (2023, November 27). *The Loch Ness monster: myth or reality?* Colorado Arts and Sciences Magazine. https://www.colorado.edu/asmagazine/2023/11/27/loch-ness-monster-myth-or-reality

Image References

ArtTower. (2018). Atlantis, sea, nature image [Online Image]. In *Pixabay*. https://pixabay.com/photos/atlantis-sea-ruins-water-3110079/

Charris, J. (2023). Nazca lines on rock [Online Image]. In *Pexels*. https://www.pexels.com/photo/nazca-lines-on-rock-17428661/

Crismariu, G. (2019, October 18). *Puzzled*. Unsplash. https://unsplash.com/photos/close-up-photography-of-puzzles-sOK9NjLArCw

de Jonge, M. (n.d.). *cyanideandcoffee | Jack ripper, Jack, nerd life*. Pinterest. Retrieved February 7, 2024, from https://www.pinterest.co.uk/pin/72409506516952018/

References

Dijkhof, J. (2022, September 6). *Deze 5 fascinerende programma's over mythes en legendes moet je zien*. Streamwijzer. https://www.streamwijzer.nl/mythes-legendes-discovery-plus/

Jack the ripper | fantasy landscape, dark art, gothic art. (n.d.). Pinterest. Retrieved February 7, 2024, from https://www.pinterest.co.uk/pin/37436240627285085/

Jurik, N. (2018). Stonehenge, megalith, monument image [Online Image]. In *Pixabay*. https://pixabay.com/photos/stonehenge-megalith-monument-3193407/

monikawl999. (2015). Nasca, Peru, Nasca plateau image [Online Image]. In *Pixabay*. https://pixabay.com/photos/nasca-peru-nasca-plateau-1089342/

Nothing Ahead. (2021). Spotlight on a map [Online Image]. In *Pexels*. https://www.pexels.com/photo/spotlight-on-a-map-9494912/

Parizo, Y. (n.d.). *Roanoke island colony | halloween art, halloween artwork, creepy pictures*. Pinterest. Retrieved February 7, 2024, from https://www.pinterest.co.uk/pin/18929260927510335/

Perry, M. (2020, July 24). *The 15th century Voynich Manuscript and the naked women*. 67 Not Out. http://www.67notout.com/2020/07/the-15th-century-voynich-manuscript-and.html?spref=pi

Phips. (n.d.). *Épinglé par Jean Bambi sur sainte face de jesus | Saint suaire, Linceul de turin, Images religieuses*. Pinterest. Retrieved February 7, 2024, from https://www.pinterest.co.uk/pin/152418768631086275/

Pixabay. (2016). The great sphinx [Online Image]. In *Pexels*. https://www.pexels.com/photo/the-great-sphinx-262786/

Romanova, A. (2023a, November 4). *A beautiful table clock in the Amder Room of the Catherine Palace*. Unsplash. https://unsplash.com/photos/a-clock-sitting-on-top-of-a-table-in-a-room-tBzRhIjjHP4

Romanova, A. (2023b, November 4). *The angels in the corner of the amber room in the catherine palace*. Unsplash. https://unsplash.com/photos/a-gold-painted-room-with-a-chandelier-and-candles-cZGrLJ2kjtk

Shershaby, M. E. (2020). Ancient stone pyramids in dry sandy desert [Online Image]. In *Pexels*. https://www.pexels.com/photo/ancient-stone-pyramids-in-dry-sandy-desert-3772783/

Tasi, Z. (2019, March 29). *Photo by Zoltan Tasi on Unsplash*. Unsplash. https://unsplash.com/photos/gray-boat-on-brown-sand-2pQk8FPOK1s

Walkerssk. (2018). Stonehenge, monolith, monoliths image [Online Image]. In *Pixabay*. https://pixabay.com/photos/stonehenge-monolith-monoliths-3160614/

Walsh, M. (2020, July 22). *Question mark painted on a brick wall*. Unsplash. https://unsplash.com/photos/text-tVkdGtEe2C4